The Art of Presenting

Getting it right in the post-modern world

Alan Gillies

Radcliffe Publishing

Oxford ● New York

Radcliffe Publishing Ltd
18 Marcham Road
Abingdon
Oxon OX14 1AA
United Kingdom

www.radcliffe-oxford.com
Electronic catalogue and worldwide online ordering facility.

British Library Cataloguing in Publication Data

A catalogue record for this book is available from the British Library.

ISBN-10: 1 84619 091 6
ISBN-13: 978 1 84619 091 9

Typeset by Anne Joshua & Associates, Oxford
Printed and bound by TJI Digital, Padstow, Cornwall

Contents

Preface   vi
   What this book is about   vi
   Who this book is for   vi
   Why I wrote this book   vii
   About this book   viii

1 Introduction: the three eras of presentation   1
   Era 1: The pre-modern era of presentation   1
   Era 2: The modern era of presentation   2
   Era 3: The post-modern era of presentation   6

2 Ten questions to answer by planning your talk, and your answers   9
   Question 1:   How do I plan to be spontaneous?   9
   Question 2:   What is the talk about?   11
   Question 3:   Who is the talk aimed at?   12
   Question 4:   What knowledge may be assumed?   15
   Question 5:   How long should it be?   17
   Question 6:   How big can a chunk be?   20
   Question 7:   What are the key messages?   22
   Question 8:   How will you help people remember them?   23
   Question 9:   What is the take-home message?   25
   Question 10: What's in the party bag, and what shall I do with it?   25
   And so in summary: what should my plan look like?   27

3 Ten questions to answer about giving your talk   29
   Question 1:   What style should I adopt?   29
   Question 2:   What should I wear?   30
   Question 3:   Do I talk with my hands?   35
   Question 4:   Should I use humour?   37
   Question 5:   Should I use anecdotes?   40
   Question 6:   How fast should I go?   41
   Question 7:   How loudly should I talk?   43
   Question 8:   How do I reinforce my key messages without boring
            my listeners?   45
   Question 9:   How do I handle questions?   48
   Question 10: How much detail do I need to include in the talk?   50

4 Ten things to do with presentation graphics that aren't bulleted
lists that whizz in and do a quick orbit before settling down in a
font that can't be read from the front row   53

   Things to do 1: Go minimal   53
   Things to do 2: Use the graphics before and after but not during 56
   Things to do 3: Fluffy clouds   57
   Things to do 4: Build transition: explaining a process   60
   Things to do 5: Images for reinforcement   62
   Things to do 6: Take a tiered approach to detail   68
   Things to do 7: Use presentation slides as milestones or signposts 70
   Things to do 8: Repetition for reinforcement   73
   Things to do 9: Send on the warm-up act   84
   Things to do 10: Clues for non-native speakers   87

5 The take-home message   89

6 The afterword   91

The Appendix: the handouts   93

Index   109

For George Gillies
(1927–2006)

Preface

What this book is about

This book is about talking. It's one of my favourite activities. Just ask my students, friends, family and anyone else who knows me. The problem is that I believe that the art of talking, or public speaking if you prefer, is under threat from technology. Just look at what has happened to using the telephone: we have a generation growing up who prefer to use mobile phones for 'texting' rather than talking, despite the fact that as a piece of technology, a mobile phone is singularly ill-equipped for the task, hence the reason that we have to invent even cleverer technology such as predictive texting to overcome the basic limitations of the device.

The focus of this book, however, is the times when we are speaking in public, addressing a group of people. Over the years, I have found myself doing this in a wide range of situations:

- lecturing as part of my day job
- presenting research findings to my academic peers
- presenting to potential future colleagues as part of an interview process
- presenting slides of overseas projects to ladies' meetings and others
- preaching to a Methodist congregation on a Sunday.

These situations are all different, and as with many things, context is everything.

At the same time there are underlying principles that can be generalised. This book seeks to explore some of those general principles and to equip the reader to take account of their context and apply those principles in their own context.

Who this book is for

This book is for people who find themselves in situations where they have to talk to groups of people: all the kinds of situation that I have found myself in over the years.

- You may be a lecturer tired of giving the same old talk with the same old bulleted lists.
- You may be someone who's just discovered that slide projectors are much harder to get hold of and so wants to find new ways of delivering your talk.
- You may be a practitioner who wants to share your knowledge with colleagues

but remembers falling asleep at the last event you attended and wants to avoid your colleagues doing the same.
- You may be a salesperson who wants to distinguish yourself from your competitors.

And there are a few people who should read no further, for example:

- if you think that all you need for your talk is a nice presentation, or
- if you think that there's absolutely nothing wrong with 40 identical slides with the logo in precisely the same place and the words precisely the same shade of navy blue, or
- if you believe that what you have to say is so interesting that no one could possibly not be interested in it, too, or
- if you are not interested in having your views challenged

then please save yourself the effort of reading the rest of the book.

Why I wrote this book

I wrote this book because I was fed up. Actually, to be precise I wrote a chapter of a book several years ago because I was fed up. The book was *Presenting Health with PowerPoint*. It contains what I shall characterise in this book as the modernist view of public speaking, and it told people how to use PowerPoint. However, perhaps as an act of rebellion against the modernist view, I included a chapter entitled 'How not to ruin your talk with PowerPoint'. By the time I'd finished this was the most important chapter in the book for me. This book is an expansion and development of those thoughts.

 Pause for thought

Think about the last talk you listened to.

1 Was it interesting?
2 What do you remember from it?
3 What was the main point of the talk?
4 Have you done anything differently as a result of the talk?

Or if you are feeling brave try the more courageous version.

 **Pause for thought**

Think about the last talk you gave.

1 Was it interesting?
2 What do you remember from it?
3 What was the main point of the talk?
4 Have you done anything differently as a result of the talk?

About this book

This book is organised in three main sections, planning, delivery and things you might do with the technology that are not bulleted lists.

Throughout the book you will find details that are meant to reflect what the book is trying to do. You will find illustrations and cartoons that are designed to do what they say on the tin, illustrate a point through an image. You will find examples that are designed to show how the principles described were implemented in a specific context.

And there is an email address provided so that you can communicate with me. Here's why you might want to do that.

• You might just want to tell me what you think: for better or for worse!
• I can supply templates and other resources in support of specific examples.
• There are places where I refer to websites. The trouble is, that if I include the web address it will disappear: previous experience shows 25% of web addresses change in the time it takes to write and publish a book. So if you want a web address, send me an email.
• You might want to share your own good practice.

To send me an email, send it to talking@alangillies.com.
Where you see the 'email me' icon:

Email me!

there are extra resources available for those who email me.

 **Pause for thought**

You have already seen an example of the exercises you will find throughout the book to help you think about the content.

 Where you see this icon look for a footnote at the bottom of the page.

If we can get enough interest, we will set up a community of good practice to share ideas. Will it happen? I don't know! That is the joy and frustration of working in a post-modern way. But if you don't contact me you'll never know.

Alan Gillies
January 2007

Footnotes provide information that may detract from the flow of the main text, so is placed at the bottom of the page. Still, I think they're worth reading, or else I wouldn't have put them in there in the first place.

1 Introduction: the three eras of presentation

Era 1: The pre-modern era of presentation

In the good old days, we are told that public speakers could produce oratory that would hold the attention of people for hours on end without any recourse to artificial aids whatsoever. As with most nostalgic visions of a golden age in the past, it is only partially true.

There is good evidence of the power of the great orators. The good: Martin Luther King captured on film in 1963 at the Lincoln Memorial speaking to 250,000 people with his 'I have a dream' speech; the bad: Adolf Hitler, spreading hatred through his oratory in the 1920s and 1930s; and the short: John Wesley, the Oxford don, just 5 foot 3 inches tall going out to preach to the illiterate miners of Bristol and attracting nearly 8,000 on his first Sunday alone in April 1739.

Email me! Some of the great oratory of the twentieth century has been captured on film and has been made available on the Internet. Contact me for details of where to see Martin Luther King's 1963 speech for example.

On the other hand, this view belongs to the same golden age where the local bobby cycled around preventing local youths from becoming drugs barons by a simple clip around the ear. For every great orator, we can remember the occasions when we have been bored to tears. I remember being on a course for new lecturers where we were learning about teaching, and a colleague announced: 'Well the problem is, I have the most boring part of the syllabus to teach!' This was almost certainly a self-fulfilling prophecy! I was glad I wasn't one of his students.

Graphics to accompany talks were either hand written, typed or photographic slides. The overhead projector allowed speakers to illustrate their talks with words and sketches in hideous shades of mauve.

Viewed from the present, much of the activity of even 20 years ago looks hideously old-fashioned. There are almost certainly increased expectations on the part of listeners these days. Many people are seeking to communicate with them in very sophisticated ways. Today's children live in a world of instant, high-quality media. We are also dealing with a much less deferential society. In many cases, listeners will not sit still to be politely bored, and if they do it once, they will do it no more than once.

As an undergraduate, I was part of a group of 180 students. For the first week of a lecture course it was normal for about 100 students to turn up. Over the next few weeks the numbers either rose to about 120 as good reports spread, or started to drop. There was one lecturer who was rumoured to have been very close to receiving a Nobel prize. However, his lecturing style was such that by week 5 there were only 11 students left. Two weeks later, he was into single figures apparently. I cannot speak from first hand because I had given up by that point.

Some readers may be shocked by this and feel that more pressure should have been exerted to make attendance compulsory. Apart from the flippant observation that human rights conventions were introduced to stop such abuse, surely the more appropriate response is to seek to improve the quality of communication. There's no point in enforcing attendance if no communication takes place. And students did attend if they felt it was worthwhile.

Another lecturer had written a book based on his lectures: it was sufficiently close to the content of the lectures that at the end of each session you could agree with colleagues that he had reached the bottom of page X. And yet he achieved very good attendance because his lectures added understanding to the written word on the page.

Characteristic of this era of presentation was a great variation in the quality of public speaking. The best was wonderful, the worst was truly awful.

Pause for thought

As with many other activities, the computer has revolutionised the way that we do public speaking.

- What do you think are the advantages?
- What do you think are the disadvantages?

Era 2: The modern era of presentation

One response to this problem is to use presentation graphics software to provide a presentation to illustrate the talk, and maybe give out hand-outs of the slides as an aide memoire. Unfortunately, this superficially attractive theory does not stand up in practice.

There is a truism in IT (information technology) that if you introduce computers into a situation that is well organised, understood and structured, then a properly designed and implemented IT system will make things better. By contrast, a situation that may be characterised as disorganised will remain disorganised at best, and in many cases, the disorder will be multiplied by the introduction of IT.

Thus a disorganised and unclear talk is likely to be illustrated by slides that are cluttered and incomprehensible. A boring talk is usually accompanied by even more boring slides!

A computer with a presentation graphics package is a tool. Think about digging a hole in the road. Is a pneumatic drill a better tool than a pick and shovel? Well that depends. It's a more powerful tool, but it all depends on what you are going to do with it. If you are skilled in its use, it will undoubtedly speed up your task. If you're as clumsy as I am, and whatever you use is as likely to make a hole in your foot as the road, then the more powerful tool will simply do more damage. If you think this is a foolish example, then consider the following ways in which presentation graphics packages can add to the portfolio of sure-fire ways to ruin your talk, all of which I have seen.

- The speaker who has no concept of time management can now add the crime of producing far too many slides, thus ensuring that they run over time, and that anyone with a hand-out will know in advance that they don't stand a chance of sticking to time.
- The speaker who cannot structure a talk is unlikely to suddenly acquire the skill of structuring a slide, and will often produce spectacularly cluttered slides.
- The speaker who prizes uniformity above all and speaks in the same dull monotone will likely produce screen after screen of uniform bulleted lists, which will only serve to reinforce the complete lack of variation in the whole presentation.

And I could go on, but you would quickly become bored with my bulleted list. When I sit in the audience of such talks, I am reminded of a song I learnt in childhood.

 Little boxes on the hillside, little boxes made of ticky tacky.
Little boxes, little boxes, little boxes all the same.
There's a green one and a pink one and a blue one and a yellow one,
And they're all made out of ticky tacky, and they all look just the same.
Malvina Reynolds

 The illustrations used in this book are available in colour from the author as a PowerPoint presentation.

Email me!

And I can't help thinking of a version for today's presenters:

Little lists made up of bullets, little lists made out of tittle tattle.
Lists of bullets, lists of bullets, lists of bullets all the same.
There's a logo and a title and a bullet and another one,
And they're all made out of tittle tattle, and they all look just the same!
With apologies to Malvina Reynolds

 I'm afraid asides are something of a characteristic of my verbal style, so they crop up in the book as footnotes like this. The song 'Little Boxes' was allegedly written about Levittown, Pennsylvania. During the course of my research for this book (Yes, I did some!) I came across a website all about it. If you want the URL, just email me!

"By contrast, a situation which may be characterised as disorganised will remain disorganised at best, and in many cases, the disorder will be multiplied by the introduction of IT"

Just as enforcing attendance at my undergraduate lectures would not have improved communication and could have made matters worse by making the audience restive and the lecturer nervous, so giving people powerful tools without sorting out the underlying issues is a bad idea. It is the presentation equivalent of giving me a pneumatic drill!

To improve the quality of talks, you must first sort out the fundamentals of presentation: check that you as the speaker have a grasp of how to plan a talk, structure a talk and deliver a talk. Having established the fundamentals, it is likely that you will be able to enhance your talk with the appropriate tools and avoid the equivalent of shooting (or drilling!) yourself in the foot.

If you think about other arenas, then first we learn the rules to guide us on how to act competently. However, if we wish to progress beyond competence to expertise, then a key skill we need to learn is how to use judgement on when to go beyond the rules.

Consider a model of how we move from being a novice to an expert, adapted from the work of first Dreyfus and Dreyfus (1980), refined by Benner (1984) and Storey *et al.* (2002) (*see* Table 1.1). A novice operates under instruction, a proficient person performs according to rules and processes. The mark of an expert is someone who knows when to break the rules to good effect.

Table 1.1 Moving from novice to expert: it's more than just obeying the rules

Level	Description
Level 0	This does not form a part of the current or future role of the worker
Level 1 – Foundation	The practitioner would work under the direct supervision of others more proficient in this competency. (This level of attainment may apply to the practitioner gaining experience and developing skills and knowledge in the competency.)
Level 2 – Intermediate	The practitioner can demonstrate acceptable performance in the competency and has coped with enough real situations in the workplace to require less supervision and guidance, but they are not expected to demonstrate full competence or practise autonomously.
Level 3 – Proficient	A practitioner who consistently applies the competency standard. The practitioner demonstrates competence through the skills and ability to work effectively without the need for direct supervision. (The proficient practitioner may practise autonomously, and supervise others, within a restricted range of competences.)
Level 4 – Advanced	The advanced practitioner is autonomous and reflexive, perceives situations as wholes, works accurately and is aware of current best practice. Advanced practitioners understand a situation as a whole because they perceive its meaning in terms of long-term goals. (The advanced practitioner is likely to be leading a team; delivering and supervising delivery, evaluating the effectiveness of practice being delivered and may also contribute to the education and training of others.)
Level 5 – Expert	The expert practitioner is able to demonstrate a deeper understanding of the situation and contributes to the development and dissemination of knowledge through the teaching and development of others. The expert practitioner is likely to have their own caseload and provide advice, guidance and leadership to other professionals.

The use of technology and the following of standard rules will raise novices to the level of proficiency and prevent some of the worst excesses. However, it will take you no further, and proficiency in public speaking can quickly become rather tedious.

In the modernist era, mindful of how often we fail to produce a talk of any aesthetic merit at all, we have emphasised consistency as the measure of quality. Rules are defined in an attempt to eliminate the worst excesses. In terms of the model in Table 1.1, such rules will help to move people from novice to proficient performer. In the process, talks become much more uniform and individual creativity may be stifled. The novice may be raised to proficiency, but the chance to exhibit true expertise is lost. And while one proficient talk may be OK to listen to, a whole day of the merely proficient quickly degenerates into the merely boring.

Rules tend to be defined in the negative:

- don't talk too quickly
- don't have too many slides in your talk
- don't wave your arms around

and so on. They resemble the Ten Commandments, which the observant reader will notice are located in the very early stages of the Bible, in the book of Exodus. Around about 10 books later, the Biblical writers start to grapple with a view of the world that seeks to move beyond simply prohibiting the negative. Although this thinking dates from about 1000BC, it is perhaps the first attempt to move seriously beyond a rigid, systemised orthodoxy.

In our terms, we define the era of rules, systemisation and technology as modernism. Therefore, logically, what follows may be described as 'post-modernist'.

Era 3: The post-modern era of presentation

When I suggested this book, and its title, it was the post-modern bit that got everybody's attention. The trouble is, for at least half of them it got up their nose as well. That's the trouble with doing something that gets you noticed, it can be counter-productive. I have witnessed presentations that subscribe to the Oscar Wilde view:

The only thing worse than being talked about is not being talked about.

Oscar Wilde

and frankly they become tiresome fairly quickly. On the other hand, if you do not engage the attention of your audience, then you will not communicate your messages and you are wasting your time.

Taken from *The Hitchhiker's Guide to the Galaxy*, Douglas Adams, 1978, Pan Books, London.

The definition of post-modernism (if such a thing is not an oxymoron) that I am using is:

> Of or relating to art, architecture, or literature that reacts against earlier modernist principles, as by reintroducing traditional or classical elements of style or by carrying modernist styles or practices to extremes.
>
> *Source: The American Heritage*[R] *Dictionary of the English Language,* Fourth Edition. © 2004, 2000 Houghton Mifflin Company.

In this case, I believe that there is an emerging approach to public speaking that is in direct reaction to the unthinking and uncritical use of presentation graphics. If we characterise such use as modernism, then it becomes logical to characterise the emergent ideas as 'post-modern'.

The ability to know when to follow the rules, and when not to, or how to deal with the situation not covered by the rules, is what defines an expert in the novice to expert model. These are the people whose talks you will remember, who will leave you feeling inspired about their subject. The mark of the truly great speaker is that you want to go and hear them talk, irrespective of the subject, just for the pleasure of hearing them talk.

One of the central propositions of this book is that merely following the rules of good presentation will produce competent but dull talks. One competent talk may be OK, but a programme made up of competent but dull talks quickly becomes very boring.

A secondary theme of this book is the importance of non-verbal communication in public speaking. Everything we do sends out messages: our dress, body language, speed of speech. The inclusion of the term 'post-modern' in the title sends out the message that public speaking is essentially an art form, not a science. It is a creative process, not about following a recipe. On the other hand, this is not an excuse for a lack of planning, as we shall see in the next section.

In Table 1.2, I compare some of the characteristics of modernist and post-modernist approaches to public speaking.

Table 1.2 Characteristics of modernist and post-modern approaches to public speaking

Modernist approach	Post-modernist approach
• Emphasises uniformity • Uses presentation graphics universally • Emphasises need to cover the material • Seeks to communicate as much as possible • Principally a logical positive process • Benefits from planning	• Emphasises variety • Uses presentation graphics sparingly for specific purposes • Emphasises key points; may use follow-up written material to cover additional material • Seeks to engage the listener as much as possible • Principally a creative process • Degenerates into a complete mess without planning!

You will have correctly established by now that I perceive myself to be in the post-modernist camp. This dates back to an incident when one of my former students went to work for a friend of mine, unaware of the connection. When quizzed about my lectures, he went on at great length and detail about what was in my lectures, and what he thought was wrong with them. When asked about colleagues' lectures, he replied that he didn't remember much about them.

It seems self-evident that if you engage your listeners, you may upset, irritate or just confuse them. On the other hand, if you don't engage their interest, your attempt to communicate seems doomed to failure before you have started.

Pause for thought

Think about the talks that you have attended in the last year.

1   How many do you remember?
2   How many do you actually remember what was said?
3   How many inspired a distinct emotion, such as irritation, enthusiasm, anger?
4   Have you heard a speaker who made you feel that you wanted to hear them speak again, irrespective of the topic?

So will you become an expert speaker just by reading this book? Probably not. Expertise is based on experience as well as knowledge. The post-modernist view will take you beyond the rules, but you need to replace them with something. This book will provide you with some knowledge to start that process. After that, it's down to you!

2 Ten questions to answer by planning your talk, and your answers

Question 1: How do I plan to be spontaneous?

Some of the best speakers are those who appear to be speaking in a spontaneous fashion. For the speaker who wishes to read his presentation from notes or a script, planning is essential. For the person who wishes to appear more spontaneous, planning is even more essential.

Pause for thought

Planning is about knowing what you are doing and what you are trying to achieve. One way to plan is to answer a series of questions. Think about the last time you spoke in public. Did you know the answers to the following questions?

1 What was the talk about?
2 Who was it aimed at?
3 What knowledge did you assume that the listeners had before you started?
4 How long was it meant to be?
5 How long was it actually?
6 What were the key points that you wanted to get across?
7 How did you help people remember them?
8 What was the take-home message?
9 What did you expect people to do as a result of the talk?
10 What did you give them to take away to help them do it?

Come on, be honest: how many did you score?

0–2	Rest assured. The time you spend reading this book will not be wasted. There are lots of things you can do to improve your presentation skills.
3–7	Don't worry. You've obviously thought about quite a lot of issues, but there's plenty of scope for new ideas.
8–9	Come along for the ride. You've pretty much got it sussed: either that or you're telling fibs. Still, I hope there are enough good ideas for you to borrow in the rest of the book to make it worthwhile reading further.
10	Great minds think alike, or fools seldom differ!

When I first started standing up in front of a group to talk it was on secondary school teaching practice in an area where there was 40% unemployment due to the recent closure of the local steel works. As a raw student teacher, I needed all the help I could get just to survive. Going into those classes with a tightly defined plan with a clear aim, learning outcomes and timetable for activities gave you a fighting chance of survival, as opposed to a slim chance of surviving the fight. Without such a plan you were lost before you started.

The first time I presented to an audience of higher education lecturers, as part of a job interview, the sense of relief that the worst that could happen was that they would politely nod off was palpable, and in sharp contrast to the anxieties of my other interviewees. On the other hand, perhaps if academic conference attendees threw things at the speakers when they were bored, then such presenters might be tempted to sharpen up their act.

I don't think that presentation graphics packages have helped us at all in this respect. They encourage speakers to sit down in front of their computers and think 'What do I want to say today?', and start typing. There is a clear temptation to rush to type, to use a kind of prototyping approach to planning the talk.

A prototyping approach assumes that we will gradually refine the talk until we arrive at a version with which we are happy. The problem with the 'rush to type' approach is that we haven't thought about the criteria that we will use to decide whether a version is acceptable and whether a change takes us nearer the product that we want.

Consider the following analogy. If I want to get from Preston to Manchester, I know that my destination is in a south-easterly direction, and so I would head off down the motorway in that direction. Now if it were 8 o'clock in the morning, I would get stuck in the rush hour traffic. So I might try a couple of alternative strategies: take the train or use the A roads to try and dodge the jams. However, if I don't think it through, I might make changes for the worse: for example, try the express coach, which would be slower and would get stuck in the same jams because it uses the same motorway; or worse still, drive off in completely the wrong direction, because I haven't got a clear idea of where I'm heading.

On the other hand, if you plan your talk before you start typing, you can use the answers to the questions above to help you refine it. If you know how long it's meant to be, then you make an informed judgement about how much material you need. If you know who your audience is then you can start to make informed decisions about how much prior knowledge you may assume.

At the end of this chapter, you will find a template to help you plan your talk. Hopefully, in the rest of this chapter you will find out more about what goes in that plan.

Question 2: What is the talk about?

When prospective PhD students turn up in my office, I normally ask them what they want to study for their PhD. Generally, they talk for about 20 minutes before they take a breath, because they are enthusiastic about their subject. At this point, I try to get a word in edgeways. When I get a chance, I tell them that that's very nice, but I would like them to do something for me: complete the following statement: 'The aim of my PhD is to . . .' in one sentence of not more than 15 words, in the manner of a competition slogan. You know the sort of thing.

> To win a copy of Alan Gillies' latest book, answer the following question:
> *How many books has Alan written for Radcliffe?*
> And complete the following slogan:
> *Alan Gillies' books are a load of tosh because . . .*

The point is that most of our first ideas are imprecise and need focus. It is much easier to describe something in 20 minutes with lots of arm waving than succinctly in a simple statement. However, if a talk is to be coherent, it should have a single overall aim. From this, we may define subsidiary objectives. If we meet all of these, then we will have met our overall aim.

Consider the following aim and objectives for a talk to a group of students:

Aim:

• To communicate the purpose of the National Programme for IT in the NHS.

Objectives:

1 To review the current organisational objectives of the NHS.
2 To review IT within the NHS to date.
3 To show how IT can help deliver the organisational objectives of the NHS.
4 To review the specific goals and plans of the National Programme for IT.
5 To review with the audience what they have learnt from the talk.

Pause for thought

Think about the last talk that you gave.

- Did you have a single focused aim?
- If so, what was it?
- Did you establish clear objectives to meet that aim?
- Did you think about whether they were met?

Pause for thought

If you are reading this book, there's a good chance that you will be talking again some time soon. If you know about such a talk, then try to answer the following questions.

- What are you trying to achieve?
- What is the specific aim of the talk? (Complete in not more than 15 words.)
- What are the objectives for this talk?
  1
  2
  3
  4
  5
- How will you know whether you achieved them?

Email me!

Email me for a template that will help you with this planning activity.

Question 3: Who is the talk aimed at?

Before you speak, it is always worth working out who the talk is aimed at. This may impact on a whole range of factors:

- assumed knowledge (to which we shall return in the next section)
- conceptual level
- vocabulary
- style.

There is a temptation to assume that 'one size fits all'. This is a very dangerous assumption. While training to be a secondary school teacher, I was once involved in an experiment to measure the reading age of a chemistry textbook. Such measures are at best an approximation. However, a reading age of 19.3 for a textbook aimed at 14-year-olds might go some way to explaining why children found the subject 'hard'.

Why does this happen? The textbook concerned was written by a university lecturer, used to lecturing to 19-year-olds, not 14-year-olds.

If you prepare a talk on a computer, you can get a measure of its general readability from the computer. Readability measures are primarily based on factors such as the number of words in the sentences and the number of letters or syllables per word (i.e. as a reflection of word frequency). Two of the most commonly used measures are the Flesch Reading Ease formula and the Flesch-Kincaid Grade Level. If you have your text in Word (PC only), then follow these steps to obtain a readability score.

1   On the Tools menu, click Options, and then click the Spelling and Grammar tab.
2   Select the Check grammar with spelling check box.
3   Select the Show readability statistics check box, and then click OK.
4   On the Standard toolbar, click Spelling and Grammar.

Word provides both measures. The Flesch Reading Ease score rates text on a 100-point scale – the higher the score, the easier it is to understand the document. For most standard documents, the majority of sources suggest that you should aim for a score of approximately 60 to 70. The Flesch-Kincaid Grade Level score rates text on a US grade-school level. (Not terribly helpful to us on this side of the pond!) For example, a score of 8.0 means that an eighth grader can understand the document. For most standard documents, you should aim for a score of approximately 7.0 to 8.0.

The formula for the Flesch Reading Ease score is:

$$206.835 - (1.015 \times ASL) - (84.6 \times ASW)$$

and the formula for the Flesch-Kincaid Grade Level score is:

$$(0.39 \times ASL) + (11.8 \times ASW) - 15.59,$$

where ASL = average sentence length (the number of words divided by the number of sentences) and ASW = average number of syllables per word (the number of syllables divided by the number of words).

Please note these scores are for guidance only. Specialist vocabulary will quickly render a talk incomprehensible to the uninitiated. There is more on this in the next section.

If we accept that it is necessary to engage the attention and sympathies of the audience, then the intended target will crucially influence the levers we try to pull to achieve this. For example, suppose the purpose of the talk is to describe the benefits of IT to the National Health Service, then:

- if you are an accountant, I should be trying to show you how it can save money; it will be acceptable to use language like cost-benefit analysis, depreciation, and you will be less likely to be impressed by improved patient care, which sounds expensive
- if you are a clinician, I should be trying to show you how it can improve care for your patients, emphasising health benefits and outcomes, and trying not to reinforce prejudices that IT is generally more about saving money than helping patients
- if you are a technology junkie, then I should be trying to show you how many megabytes, teraflops and super-dooper widgets it has. Frankly, you will take it as read that IT is a good thing and that naturally the cleverer the technology, the greater the benefit to the NHS and mankind in general.

 **Pause for thought**

Think about the last time you gave a talk.

1 Who was the talk aimed at?
2 Is that who actually turned up to listen?
3 Was the audience homogeneous?
4 If not, did different listeners have different needs?
5 How did you address different needs in the audience?

 **Pause for thought**

Think about the last time you listened to a talk.

1 Did you feel that the talk was aimed at you?
2 Was the audience full of people like you?
3 Did you think that the listeners had different needs?
4 Did the speaker do anything to take account of the different needs of different listeners?

 I'm aware that the use of 'mankind' may be regarded as non-inclusive language. However, I've never yet met a female technology junkie. At the risk of upsetting just about everybody, the technology junkie does seem to be a pretty male domain. This illustrates a serious point. In reality, we cannot produce a talk tailored to the needs and prejudices of everyone in the room. In planning, we make assumptions about the likely knowledge and values of the audience. This has inherent risks in misjudging your audience and potentially causing offence.

So what should you do?

1   Try to find out the nature of your listeners.
2   If you don't know your listeners well, don't assume too much.
3   If you have a diverse group of listeners, think about using pre-reading or hand-outs to address the needs of different listeners.
4   If you get it wrong, apologise!

Question 4: What knowledge may be assumed?

A key part of tailoring your talk to your audience is deciding what knowledge may be assumed. It can cause problems if you assume that the audience shares your knowledge and understanding of:

- key concepts
- vocabulary and terminology
- abbreviations and acronyms.

Pause for thought

Think about the last time you listened to a talk. Consider your level of prior knowledge. For the purposes of that talk:

1   were you a novice, an expert or something in between?
2   did the speaker use language that you didn't understand?
3   did the speaker use abbreviations or acronyms with which you were unfamiliar?
4   did the speaker spend a lot of time explaining things you already knew?
5   did the speaker get your level of prior knowledge about right?

Some concepts may appear self-evident to you. However, the audience may not understand the concept or may take a different view. For example, the concept of 'evidence' to a specialist in evidence-based medicine brings with it assumptions about the type of evidence and its value in terms of the hierarchy of evidence.

The statement that decisions should be based on evidence appears to be a self-evident no-brainer. However, a general practitioner may well bring together a wide range of factors, e.g. knowledge of the patient, their family history, experience, judgement, very few of which would be classified as 'evidence' in the narrow, specialised terminology of the evidence-based specialist.

This is not the place to make a value judgement about the merits of different views of evidence. Rather, the key point from a communication perspective is that you share a common understanding of what each person means by the concept. From here you can go on to disagree violently from a position of understanding exactly what you disagree about!

Similarly, you need to share a common vocabulary to communicate. If the audience doesn't understand the words you use, they will not understand what you are trying to tell them. However, there is a worse scenario, where you use words that they recognise but they attribute a different meaning to the words than you intended. This most often happens when you use abbreviations or acronyms, but can also occur with full words. Beware in particular of North American listeners who think they share a common language with the UK; alternatively, if you are a North American reader, beware this entire text, which is written in a peculiar colloquial version of English native to the north of England.

When I first started teaching general practitioners (GPs) to use computers it was normal for the GPs to stop me early on and request that I avoid IT jargon. Within five minutes they would be happily discussing myocardial infarctions, and the tutor would be asking them to avoid medical jargon, please! As I work in health informatics, I work with both informatics and clinical specialists. This has thrown up some interesting confusions over the years through the use of abbreviations and acronyms. My favourite is AI, which usually means 'artificial intelligence' to the IT community, but 'artificial insemination' to the medical community. There are other examples: GPs will mean 'general practitioners' to the medical community, but 'Geographical Positioning Systems' to the IT community. The case of the letters may be key here, but in a verbal presentation or under the influence of computerised auto-correction facilities, such cues may be lost.

Even the abbreviation used for information technology (IT) can be context dependent. The UK NHS has consistently adopted IM&T as its abbreviation, standing for 'information management and technology'. I am not aware of any other community where this abbreviation is in common usage.

Email me! I'm aware that this is a dangerous statement to make, so if you know of another context where this is in common usage then please let me know!

In education, ICT has been commonly adopted to refer to information and communications technology. Each of these alternative abbreviations has been adopted for sensible and laudable reasons, but the end result can be confusion, if understanding is not shared. And then there's 'informatics': the term means many different things to different people. For example, if I tell you that the National Programme for IT has an informatics programme, what do you think it covers?

So, how to prevent confusion caused by abbreviations and acronyms? The convention for written documents is to explain each abbreviation on first usage. I have tried to follow this convention in this book. You can use this convention in slides to accompany a talk. However, this can get untidy on slides, which tend to be a summary, and assumes that every abbreviation used will appear on a slide (awfully constraining and modernist!). A better strategy is to provide a hand-out listing *all* the abbreviations you wish to use, including those that do not appear on the slides. It allows the user to look up an abbreviation if you use it more than once, and they missed it the first time.

Unless you are in the most formal of settings, it's usually worth inviting the listeners near the start of your talk to interrupt you if you use jargon or abbreviations that they don't understand.

 **Pause for thought**

What do you understand by the following abbreviations? They all have at least two meanings that I know of.

1 AI
2 DNA
3 NTA
4 AA
5 ASA

Question 5: How long should it be?

Gosh! This really is the proverbial length of a piece of string. The immediate answer is generally long enough to fill the time available, which will often be prescribed for you. However, the first decision you need to make is how much of the time are you going to set aside for discussion. This may be at the end of or during your talk, if you are going to allow interaction to occur during your presentation.

 **Pause for thought**

How many talks have you listened to recently where the speaker has over-run? What did you think when they did? Was it one of the following?

1 This is clearly a very important and clever person, so they should talk longer than anyone else.
2 Well it wasn't very good, but at least we got good value!
3 I wish they'd stopped 10 minutes ago, it would have been a much better talk.
4 Pity the poor person coming after them, who'll now run over into coffee time.
5 I wish the chair had kept them to time.

However, this is a crucial matter because running over your allotted time is a discourtesy to your listeners and to anyone who might be sharing the platform. It also sends out two unfortunate non-verbal messages:

1   You can't organise yourself properly: there is no more obvious manifestation of this.
2   You like the sound of your own voice too much.

It also often prevents time for discussion, which is the part of the talk where you might learn something useful.

The traditional modernist view of timekeeping is to organise your talk around no more than one slide every two minutes. Fine, but sometimes I talk about a slide for ages, and sometimes I put up an image for effect and it's gone in a couple of seconds because it's done its job.

At one university where I worked, our lecture slots were organised in two-hour slots. One of my colleagues used to love very complex overhead projector slides, and his fellow lecturers devised a unit of measurement and named it after him. A '1 ****er' slide was a slide he could talk about for an hour; the ultimate was a '2 ****er' slide – he could do a whole two-hour session from one slide.

When I left that university I found myself competing for my new job with another colleague. I knew him to be a 'one-slide-a-minute', bulleted-list man. True to form, he turned up to present to the staff in the new department with lots of slides printed out for all attendees. He dealt out the remnants of a shredded rainforest to the listeners, who all received their own personal pile of paper. I followed him. I had two slides. The first I put up at the beginning of the talk with the question on it that I had been asked to talk about. The other slide was displayed 18 minutes later and contained three key messages from the talk.

It is certainly true that many people in the modernist bulleted-list school of presenting do have too many slides. In such cases, a simple rule of thumb may be helpful such as no more than one slide every two minutes. However, a rule of thumb that might be more useful is:

> People generally prepare too much material, so when you have prepared your talk, throw away 20% to keep to time.

The one thing that works against this rule is people's tendency when nervous to speak more quickly. So, for example, you may have practised your talk and timed it at 25 minutes, but then deliver it in 19 minutes when anxious in front of your listeners. I remember watching in astonishment when one of my students managed to gabble through a talk that we had timed at 20 minutes the day before in under 10!

However, having too much material is not the answer: your listeners will feel that they have been dragged along behind an express train. It really is better to correct the underlying problems – too much material and speaking too quickly – rather than to try and let one compensate for the other.

For more experienced talkers, Gillies' First Law of the length of a verbal piece of string states:

You probably want to talk longer than they want to listen.

The second law states:

If the first law is wrong, then if you say too little, they will leave wanting more.

So what do we replace the 'two minutes a slide' rule with in our post-modern world? Well, first of all, if you accept that the slides are not the talk, but are there to support the talk, then the length of the talk is no longer directly measurable in terms of the number of slides, or vice versa. The talk should be:

1   no longer than it needs to be
and
2   no longer than you are allocated.

If the question you really want answered is 'How many slides should I prepare?', then the answer is, 'It depends'. It depends on the purpose of the slides. You can read more about using slides for different purposes in Chapter 5, but in the meantime, here's a flow chart to give you some ideas.

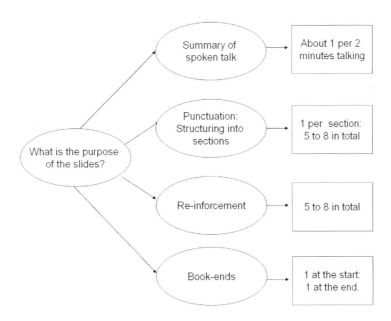

How many slides do I need?

How long should it be?

Question 6: How big can a chunk be?

Talks are generally delivered in chunks. That's why people like to use presentation graphics slides as a guide: it helps them chunk their talk and decide where one chunk stops and another starts.

Developments in media are all geared towards smaller and smaller chunks. Politicians are often accused of neglecting carefully constructed arguments for the pithy and memorable sound-bite. In spite of this, a common problem is that people try to cram too much into each chunk. This produces a number of problems, which can be identified in the following symptoms.

- It makes talks too long.
- It means that people produce too many presentation graphics slides.
- It means that individual slides become too busy.

This has led people working within a modernist environment to suggest rules for presentation graphics slides. Guilty as charged, in my book on *Presenting Health with PowerPoint* you will find the following rules, which I summarised as 'less is more'.

Rule	What I said about it
Never put more than five points on one slide	If you find yourself in breach of this rule, best practice is to say less and remove some text. If not, make two slides
Keep each point short, use no more than six words per point	If you find yourself in breach of this rule, best practice is to say less and remove some text. If not, make two points
Don't have too many slides, not more than one slide per two minutes' talking (120 seconds)	If you find yourself in breach of this rule, best practice is to say less and remove a slide or two
Don't use more than two fonts, and don't mix serif and sans serif fonts	Times New Roman is an example of a serif font, Arial is an example of a sans serif font
Do not use all the same case, as it's easier to read a mixture of upper and lower case	This should be easier to read than THIS TEXT WHICH IS IN UPPER CASE or this text which is in lower case
Keep diagrams simple	Complex diagrams are illegible. They often include text which is too small in upper or lower case, and are offered with the feeble excuse 'I know you can't read this at the back' (*if you knew that, why did you include it – do you hate people who sit on the back row or something?*)
Avoid bright colours	Subtlety is a virtue. (Not always encouraged by PowerPoint!) Avoid bright colours, especially in large expanses, as they can be distracting, tiring and irritating to viewers
Avoid busy backgrounds	Complex background patterns can seem like a good idea but can be extremely harmful! At best they can be distracting and at worst they can completely obliterate the message. If you don't like a flat background, why not use a graded background?
Don't have too many whizzy transitions	Animation is great fun, but too much can become wearying very quickly

The case for the rules is simple. The number of talks ruined by breaching one or in some cases all of these is huge, and I doubt that you have been lucky enough to avoid one or more. However, even at the time of writing, a touch of post-modernism was present, since the next section dealt with how and when to break the rules. The fundamental problem is not a technology one. It is about the talk itself. A cluttered slide is a symptom of a cluttered talk.

A slide dominated by too many whizzy transitions is a victory for style over substance, a case of using technology because you can and because it's there. Sort out the talk, let the talking drive the presentation and the slides will take care of themselves.

A key test of an accessible web page is whether the page content is still accessible without the style sheet, which should hold all the formatting information. You can test this by switching off the style sheet. In the same way, an accessible talk should still work without any of the visual enhancements. Enhancements should do what they say on the tin: enhance. You can test this by listening to a talk with your eyes shut. It should be harder to follow, but not impossible.

- If it is easier to follow with your eyes shut, then the slides are actually getting in the way, and should be eliminated.
- If it is harder to follow but not impossible, then the slides can enhance the talk.
- If it is impossible to follow with your eyes shut, then the talk is very likely beyond salvation by slides of any kind.
- And if you fall asleep when you shut your eyes, either the talk is just plain boring or you went to too good a party last night.

Question 7: What are the key messages?

You will no doubt craft your talk as a logical argument and expect your listeners to hang on to your every word. Unfortunately, although people believe that they talk like this, people don't hear like this. People will remember the key points of your talk and some general things about it. If you don't have a logical flow to the talk and they can't follow it, they will let their attention wander. However, even if their attention doesn't wander, they will only retain a selection of messages from the whole. It is important that they retain the parts that you want them to.

This is one of the problems with amusing anecdotes. Unless they have a clear purpose and a clear message attached, they may serve as a distraction. Your listeners may go away remembering the anecdote rather than the message behind it. Therefore, you need to decide in advance what your key messages are, and design your talk around them. Illustrations, whether images, charts or anecdotes, need to reinforce these key messages rather than distract from them. Each key message – and there should not be too many – should represent a mini-peak in the talk.

Think of it as a walk (definitely not a ramble!) through the countryside. If you stay down in the valley, the walk will be flat and uninteresting. A more interesting walk will take you up into the hills. At various stages on your walk, you will reach a peak. This will almost certainly be followed by a dip, which serves to emphasise the peak. However, the next peak will also be visible until you reach the final summit at the end of your talk.

If you have too many key messages, they will no longer be key messages, they will be lost. Similarly, if you try to reinforce too much material through images or similar, their impact will be lost. Key messages have a purpose. You want your audience to do something with them. To ask more questions about them, explore further, change their practice.

 **Pause for thought**

Think of a talk that you have listened to recently.

1   What do you think were the key messages?
2   What steps did the speaker take to emphasise and reinforce them?
3   How many were there?
4   Did this seem too many to remember, or too few to make the talk worth remembering?

Question 8: How will you help people remember them?

The key points of your talk may be reinforced in a number of ways.

Visual reinforcement

Throughout this book you will find illustrations, both images and cartoons. They serve to reinforce the key messages of the text. Visual images are a powerful way of reinforcing a key point. In an ideal world, the image is powerful enough to make the point without additional words. Where words are required, the fewer needed to make the point, the bigger impact they will have.

Traditionally in the modernist era, the visual reinforcement has been through the use of literalist images as part of the presentation graphics. In a more post-modernist presentation, there is scope for both images that are more abstract and for the use of physical objects.

Verbal reinforcement

We can use a variety of ways to reinforce key messages within the talk itself. Changes in pitch, volume and pace can always be used as reinforcement, as can the dramatic pause. If a story or anecdote is to be used, it should be no longer than necessary, otherwise it becomes a distraction. A succinct quotation is often effective: a rambling anecdote hardly ever so. Humour should be used with care (*see* Question 4 in Chapter 3).

Active reinforcement

It is sometimes possible to reinforce a key point by a physical action. As always, less is more, and such physical actions should be used sparingly. I confess that I am prone to a fair amount of arm waving: this may convey energy and enthusiasm, but is too frequent to be used for reinforcement.

Active reinforcement may include demonstrations or experiments. It may include video recordings. For example, if you were talking about how a team functions you might show a video of a team in action.

The action may be on the part of your listeners. You may get them to participate in an exercise to reinforce a key point. With people's attention spans shrinking to the size of a gnat (allegedly), getting them involved is a device which may be usefully employed in almost any communication situation.

 **Pause for thought**

Think about the last advertising hoarding that you drove past that you actually remember. What do you remember?

1   The words?
2   An image?
3   The colour scheme?

Do you remember what it was advertising?

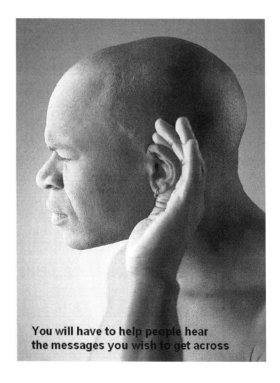

You will have to help people hear the messages you wish to get across

Question 9: What is the take-home message?

Have you ever thought of talks as fast-food drive-throughs? You drive through the talk. You pick up the messages and go away. Most of the fast food is the packaging. You discard this almost immediately. You consume the food, and most of that is gone quickly too, often leaving you hungry again. Fast food is rarely a memorable experience.

How much do you expect people to remember from your talk afterwards? Next week? Next month? Almost certainly, people will remember less than you think, and definitely less than you might hope for! Worse, left to their own devices, people tend to remember the asides, the illustrations and not the key message. However, people tend to remember the last thing they heard. This is your best opportunity to influence what your listeners remember, so don't waste it. Here is my 10-point guide to the take-home message.

1 Decide the one key message that you would choose for your listeners to remember if they forgot everything else.
2 This is your take-home message.
3 Ingrain it upon your memory: if you can't remember it, how will your listeners?
4 Keep it short: avoid 'and ninthly . . .'.
5 Make sure that the evidence for the take-home message is in your talk, but keep the declaration of the message uncluttered with justifications.
6 If the audience can't see that the take-home message arises from the talk, then there is likely to be more wrong than the take-home message itself!
7 The take-home message may be emphasised through delivery by change in tone and speed. It should stand without further reinforcement.
8 Because you want to finish with the take-home message, if you need to do an Oscar style 'I wish to thank my wife, children, cat, assistants, co-workers, manager, listeners, favourite rock band, sausage supplier' acknowledgement, then do it at the beginning before getting to the meat of the talk.
9 A simple 'thank you' at the end acts as an indication that you have stopped, without, hopefully, distracting from the take-home message.
10 The take-home message should be the last thing in your talk. This is the take-home message here!

Question 10: What's in the party bag, and what shall I do with it?

Although you may think that the take-home message is the final word on the subject, there is one further issue to think about.

Anyone with young children knows that a key part of any children's party is the party bag for the children to take away at the end of the party. Gone are the days of a piece of cake in a pretty napkin. The contents of said party bag can make or break a child's social standing for the next three months with their peers. Sad, isn't it?

The key point for us here, is that the key test is what the listener does with the contents of our party bag, the take-home message. Do they throw away the message, or treasure it? What do you as the speaker expect them to do with it?

The purpose of the talk may simply have been to inform. However, even in such a case it would be usual to hope that some listeners might have been enthused enough to seek out more information on the topic. Did you facilitate this in your talk? Did you point out places where they could find more information?

If the purpose was to get people to do something, e.g. quit smoking, stop beating their wife, adopt a llama for a village in the Andes, again did you provide them with information about what to do next, did you help them set goals and milestones if the action was not in a single step? To borrow an illustration from one of the classic public speakers of all time, you may have sown the seed of an idea, but if you don't provide instructions for its care and nurture, then the idea will likely never grow, or wither quickly away (adapted from St Matthew's Gospel, Chapter 13: 3–9).

You may find it helpful when planning your talk to consider the following diagram, adapted from a framework produced by Prof Nimal Jayaratna, which is known as NIMSAD. I have chosen the name DIMSOD for this derivative version. The name derives from a student enquiry about NIMSAD, where the student, unable to remember the name of NIMSAD said to their tutor: 'Oh you know, that framework, DIMSOD!'

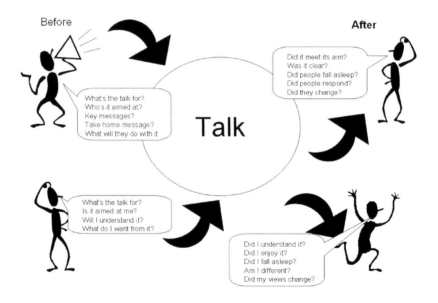

✎ Many thanks to Dr Peter Clare for the story of the forgetful student! And apologies to Prof Nimal Jayaratna for taking a rather frivolous view of NIMSAD.

The point of the diagram is to represent the talk as an engagement between a speaker and a listener. Each of them will have a state before and after the talk. Before the talk, the speaker is planning the talk and hopefully considering the questions such as those shown. Afterwards, they should be reflecting on the talk and seeking answers to questions such as those shown. The listener will have different questions, both from those they started with and those of the speaker.

And so in summary: what should my plan look like?

Now we have dealt with these issues, you should be able to draw up a plan for your talk. It may seem strange in a book that alleges a post-modernistic approach that we start with a plan. However, as stated at the beginning, if you want to appear spontaneous, you need to be twice as well planned as sticking to a rigid plan. Also, to produce a talk that communicates effectively, you need to understand the characteristics of your listeners.

Here's a template to help you plan your talk.

 You can get a copy by emailing me.

Email me!

Issue	Answer for your talk
What is the aim of the talk?	
What are your objectives?	
Who is the target audience?	
What knowledge may be assumed?	
How long should it be?	
How many sections/ chunks of knowledge should there be?	
What are the key messages?	
What is the take-home message?	
What do you expect your listeners to do with the talk?	

3 Ten questions to answer about giving your talk

Question 1: What style should I adopt?

Matching the style of your talk to your listeners is important. You will always have some leeway to impose your own style, but you must also meet the needs and expectations of your audience.

Consider style as a Venn diagram.

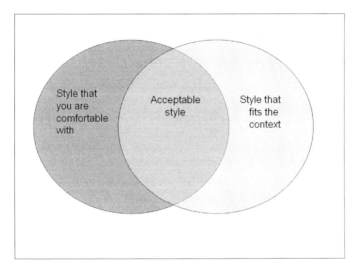

If the style doesn't fit the situation, your listeners will be uncomfortable and likely to be easily distracted, or worse, not take you seriously. Equally, you must be comfortable with the style or you will not be able to deliver your message.

Style is made up of many things. Factors that contribute to the overall style of a presentation include the following.

- *Appearance and clothing.* First impressions are important, and your appearance and clothing will speak before you do.
- *Body language and degree of movement.* The way you stand and move while speaking will both send out messages and reinforce or distract from the credibility of your message.
- *Humour.* Humour can be a powerful weapon in your armoury, but may also explode in your face. Beware the rambling anecdote!
- *Reinforcement.* You may reinforce your message with a variety of devices and evidence. What works is highly context dependent.

- *Pace.* Getting pace right is crucial. Most people benefit from slowing down. Less is more!

Just how fast should I go?

- *Volume.* Can people hear you? If they can hear the start of the sentence can they hear the last word?
- *Level of detail.* How much detail should you include? Too much and you will send your listeners to sleep – too little and your talk will appear superficial.

In this chapter, we shall seek to explore these issues in more detail by considering a set of key questions about our talk.

Question 2: What should I wear?

Does it matter? I'm afraid so, and that's just the tip of the iceberg. As noted earlier, before you open your mouth you have already sent out a whole range of non-verbal messages.

For advice in this area you can do no better than view the second episode of the BBC TV comedy series *Yes Prime Minister*, 'The Ministerial Broadcast'.

The practice session for the ministerial broadcast turns out to be a learning experience for Jim Hacker. Godfrey, the television producer, gives him all sorts of advice on how to sit, what clothes to wear, the way he should talk, etc. In the event he has nothing to say, Godfrey advises that Jim Hacker should wear a modern suit and the background should be yellow wallpaper, abstract paintings and Stravinsky as opening music. In fact, everything to disguise the fact that the speech contains nothing new. If, on the other hand, Hacker has something radical to say, then he should wear a dark suit and the reassuring traditional background (oak panelling, leather volumes and 18th-century portraits). The opening music would then be Bach. (Adapted from the *Yes Prime Minister* files, available on-line.)

✒ The Web and self-improvement bookshelves are full of advice on what (not) to wear. The reality is that much of it is common sense. For example:

1 make sure your clothes fit
2 always look clean and neat
3 keep ultra-bright colours away from face
4 do not wear large costume jewellery
5 seek to dress just a little above the level of the audience
6 wear what is comfortable for you
7 wear clothing that gives you confidence
8 it is better to wear clothes that cover too much than clothes that do not cover enough
9 make sure your hair is clean, neat and professionally styled. Avoid styles that cover more than your forehead or that you have to brush back
10 remove facial and body piercing other than single ear jewellery; visible tattoos should be covered to avoid distraction.

> Advice from the Web, courtesy of Arizona State University.

How many would you have not thought of?

Consider the following dress styles:

Style A

✒ I'm not against checklists per se, but we need to understand their limitations. There are hundreds of modernist presenters out there who have swallowed lots of checklists and conform to all of them. And bore their audiences senseless. Oh, and remember that many on the Web are American and if you are on this side of the pond may not travel well. Checklists are designed to prevent incompetence, not promote excellence.

Style B

Style C

Style D

Pause for thought

1   Use the following scales to judge your reactions to the dress styles:

Formal	10 – 9 – 8 – 7 – 6 – 5 – 4 – 3 – 2 – 1	Informal
Authoritative	10 – 9 – 8 – 7 – 6 – 5 – 4 – 3 – 2 – 1	Lacking authority
Serious	10 – 9 – 8 – 7 – 6 – 5 – 4 – 3 – 2 – 1	Frivolous
Engaging	10 – 9 – 8 – 7 – 6 – 5 – 4 – 3 – 2 – 1	Distant
Competent	10 – 9 – 8 – 7 – 6 – 5 – 4 – 3 – 2 – 1	Incompetent

2   Which of them are suitable for the following situations:

Children's party	Style A ☐	Style B ☐	Style C ☐	Style D ☐
Business presentation	Style A ☐	Style B ☐	Style C ☐	Style D ☐
Academic lecture	Style A ☐	Style B ☐	Style C ☐	Style D ☐

The point of this exercise is that the judgements we make are dependent on a range of factors, including the context in which we make the judgements and our own prejudices.

Email me!   This exercise is available as a PowerPoint presentation. Email me for a copy.

Interestingly, the Old Testament prophets, some of the earliest recorded public speakers, used to dress to illustrate the message in what was known as 'enacted prophecy'. Jeremiah, for example, went and bought a garment variously referred to as a waistcoat, linen shorts or a belt. The precise nature of the clothing is unimportant, the point was that he used it to communicate a message. This is, I think, generally a high-risk strategy.

In my early days as a Methodist preacher, when I could have acquired a reputation as an angry young man, I adopted the opposite strategy of dressing particularly smartly when I had a radical message to impart, so as to reassure the listeners. More Jim Hacker than Jeremiah, I'm afraid. However, the effectiveness of my strategy was seen when another young preacher received complaints about his message. He was also noted for wearing shabby clothes that didn't fit and not presenting himself smartly. It wasn't so much that he hadn't read the Arizona checklist, more that he didn't think it should matter, that he should be judged on what he said not what he wore. But the listeners were never receptive to what he said because his clothes had spoken before he did. And as a minister observed:

> Alan Gillies gets away with saying much more radical things than that every week, but he does it in a suit and tie!

In most cases, therefore, conservative dress will provide a blank canvas from which you can make your presentation. Striking dress is generally likely to act as a distraction.

Question 3: Do I talk with my hands?

I do. I tried to stop, but it makes me so self-conscious that I am barely able to talk and any distractions are much better than the complete collapse of animation that happens if I try to stand absolutely still.

Talk with your hands?

Careful, the cure may be worse; stop my hands moving and the words dry up!

The problem with trying to eliminate mannerisms is that the cure can be worse than the symptoms. For example, I found the following list of possible nervous mannerisms on the Web:

- bite your fingernails
- tap your feet
- wave your hands/arms
- play with your hair
- move around a lot
- speak too fast
- speak too slowly
- become stiff

- shake/shudder
- play with objects in pockets, etc.
- make strange facial expressions
- say 'uh', 'uhm'
- tap on the table/podium
- repeat yourself
- breathe heavily
- sweat
- giggle
- dry up
- shift your eyes
- move your head around.

 **Pause for thought**

OK, how many are you prepared to own up to? If you're brave, ask your listeners, and see if they find more!

Here's the modernist analysis:

Score	Modernist interpretation
0–5	You've been on all the right courses, and have your body and self under perfect control
6–10	Considerable room for improvement here. You need to control your mannerisms
11–15	You need major help. Your mannerisms and gestures will be a major distraction to your listeners
16–20	You are possibly beyond help, and almost certainly require assistance of the medical variety

My problem is that I score a good 19/20: possibly the only one I don't do is dry up. Instead, when I run out of intelligent things to say, I just move on to unintelligent things. The saving grace is that I don't do many of them often. The real issue is how often do you distract your listeners through an inappropriate use of one of these mannerisms? This will depend on how often and how severely you indulge in them.

So while this may be a list of potential mannerisms, it is probably unhelpful. If you are trying to remember not to do all of those things, you will become a hesitant, rigid zombie. I suggest that instead of focusing on the negatives – don't do this, don't do that – we should focus on positive actions to get your listeners on side. Just as clothes communicate things about us, so do our bodily actions. Faces shout louder than words. The face can emit emotionally contagious expressions, e.g. a smiling face may prompt a spontaneous response in another person. Facial expressions show approval, encourage friendship or deceive others. Unfortunately, or perhaps fortunately, most humans are not terribly good at detecting deception.

The face is the main expresser of emotions. It displays primary emotions in unique ways. The pupils of the human eye respond variously to different circumstances. The pupil either closes or widens under fearful or friendly conditions. The movement of the eyes is a key part of facial behaviour, directing others' attention or showing surprise or happiness and other emotional displays.

Eye gaze and gaze aversion help observers to know what the speaker is up to. It is commonly believed that when someone avoids looking another person in the eye, they are not trustworthy or they are lying. In reality, cultural conditioning influences how people use their faces and eyes. Black and Asian children, for example, are often taught not to look an adult directly in the eyes.

 **Pause for thought**

Consider the following images. Which face do you associate with each of the following?

1 Stress
2 Boredom
3 Worry
4 Shock
5 Success
6 Joy

Question 4: Should I use humour?

'I say, I say, I say, how should I use humour in my presentation?'
'Carefully, and in moderation!'

There is humour in this book.

(Oh no there isn't . . .)
(Oh yes there is . . .)
(Oh no there isn't . . .)

You can have too much of a good thing (or even a bad thing, see what I mean?). Humour can become tiresome after a while if overused. Apart from irritating your listeners, never a good thing to do, constant asides can interrupt the flow of a talk (are you sure . . . yes, go away, or the reader will give up on us altogether!).

If you weren't irritated by the humour before this section, the above has been designed to show you just how irritating an excess of attempts at humour can be. But even if we follow the often repeated axiom of this book that less is more, there are still reasons why humour may not work.

In any piece of humour there are a number of elements that must be present for it to be effective. The first is a shared understanding of a situation. The 'in-joke' is never funny if you are outside of the community of people that are 'in' on the joke.

Culture can play a big part. Since 1999, a book of mine has been available only in Southeast Asia, where it has continued to sell in respectable numbers. I am slightly concerned about this, since the style is distinctly informal, and I'm sure that some of the humour contained within it must be completely lost in this different culture.

Humour generally has a target. There is generally the butt of a joke, at whose expense the joke is told. In *Stranger in a Strange Land* (1961), Heinlein argues through one of his characters that:

> I have grokked this truth, and I have searched every joke I can remember. All of them fit this pattern – not only does every joke contain some element of cruelty, but the laughter during the telling (from someone who truly 'gets' it) will occur when the height of cruelty is revealed. 🦶

Speakers often use this as a device to say to the listeners: 'I'm on the same side as you, we both share a common view of the person or group who is the butt of this joke.'

Put like this, the risk is fairly apparent. You need to be confident that your view of your listeners is correct. It is frankly a cheap device, but it can be effective. I was once asked to attend a day conference for nurses about quality at a time when the Government mantra was 'private sector good, public sector bad'. As a consequence, the first two presentations were from large commercial organisations that spent a considerable amount of time telling the audience how wonderful their organisations were. I sat among the audience and observed fidgeting, eyes drooping and heads nodding. Then we had a coffee break, during which the commercial speakers left. I was the next speaker and began my presentation with:

> So now we know how wonderful company X and company Y are, shall we talk about nursing?

It brought the house down.

Cheap shot? Yes. Effective? Yes. Justified? I think so, because the butt of the joke were the organisations, not the individuals. But the alternative view is that it was (a) high risk, and (b) discourteous to my fellow speakers. Most, if not all, humour has a butt of the joke. Obviously, humour based on race, religion and, I would suggest, anything that attacks an individual directly is unacceptable. Unfortu-

---

🦶 The word 'grok' is invented by Heinlein, and roughly translated means 'understand'.

nately, it is not always possible to provide clear guidance about where boundaries lie. And of course, there's always the danger that what you think is hilarious is simply not funny to your listeners.

Humour is dangerous! Handle with care.

Question 5: Should I use anecdotes?

The sort of self-help websites that seek to improve public speaking are often greatly in favour of anecdotes. I found the following advice on one of them.

> Anecdotes are among the most powerful communications tools ever discovered by man. Jesus used them for his teaching and we know them as parables. Abraham Lincoln used them constantly, infusing them with a wry frontier humour for which he is still remembered.
>
> Anecdotes are stories, from your own experience or someone else's, told to make a point. As a young lawyer in Illinois, Lincoln was pleading a case before a jury when he became convinced he was losing, even though right was on his side. So he told the jury this story:
>
> 'A farmer back home was sitting on his front porch,' Lincoln said, 'when suddenly his six-year-old son came running from the barn saying, "Father, Father, the hired man is in the hayloft with Big Sister. The hired man is pulling down his pants and Big Sister is lifting up her skirts, and I fear they are going to pee on the hay." "Son," said the farmer calmly. "You have all the facts right but you have reached the wrong conclusion."'
>
> The jury roared with laughter and Lincoln won his case handily.

I have no wish to take issue with a great figure from history, but the anecdote doesn't travel well across the pond. I do not share its cultural values, or even its language. It does nothing for me.

The same website offers a library of anecdotes that you can draw upon (for a fee!) to enhance your talk. One of the strengths of the effective use of anecdotes is the ability to use personal experiences to demonstrate credibility and relevance. Personally, I don't favour second-hand anecdotes.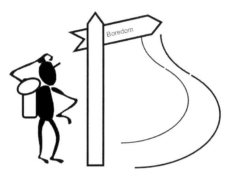

Anecdotes are like jokes. They just go on longer. Which means that the value they add to a talk must be greater than the distraction they provide from the main flow of the talk. All the things we said about humour apply to anecdotes. But there is one additional danger: the rambling anecdote. This apparently innocent device can derail the finest talk, send the most alert audience to sleep and leave even the speaker wondering what the point of it all was anyway.

Once again, the key message is 'less is more'. Short, pithy, focused anecdotes that make clear points enhance a talk by amplifying key points and linking what can be abstract points to real life. The key words here are 'short', 'pithy' and 'focused'.

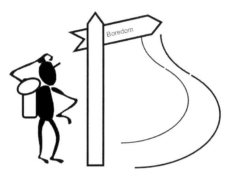

The rambling anecdote . . . Beware!

Question 6: How fast should I go?

Pace is a key part of delivery. Go too slowly and your listeners will literally be lulled to sleep. Slow delivery can be interpreted as hesitancy and does not inspire confidence. On the other hand, excessive speed will make you difficult to follow and unintelligible to people for whom your language may not be their first. In reality, although slow delivery may seem to imply hesitancy, most people need to slow down from their usual informal conversational speed when speaking in formal situations.

You should also factor in that, generally, nervous people will speed up, probably driven by a subconscious desire to get the ordeal over as soon as possible. Apparently, presenting or speaking to an audience regularly tops the list in surveys of people's top fears – more than heights, flying or dying. This has a physiological basis: a common physical reaction to having to speak in public is a release of adrenaline and cortisol into the body, the equivalent to drinking seven cups of coffee. Add actual coffee as well, and you could end up seriously hyped.

Physical relaxation techniques may also help.

Cynics who know me would say that I am an inveterate storyteller and tell so many of my own anecdotes, that to introduce others would be superfluous to requirements, and that others may be more restrained in telling of personal experiences. Judge for yourself from this book. You might think that – I couldn't possibly comment.

- Breathe deeply and slowly.
- Tighten the muscles in your toes. Hold for a count of 10. Relax and feel the sensation of release from tension.
- Flex the muscles in your feet. Hold for a count of 10. Relax.
- Move slowly up through your body – legs, abdomen, back, neck, face – contracting and relaxing muscles as you go.

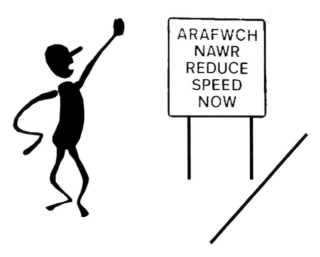

Most people benefit from slowing down – less is more!

Pause for thought

So do you talk too quickly? Here are three tests for you.

1 Tape yourself. How does it sound? Is it a comfortable pace to listen to?
2 Ask a friend what they think. I mean a real friend: someone whom you trust to be honest with you!
3 Find someone for whom English (or your native tongue) is not their first language. Ask them if they think you speak too quickly.

However, a competent speaker delivers at a pace that can be readily understood and heard, and this is emphasised within the modernist paradigm. Within my post-modernist view, an expert should be using pace as a tool to engage his listeners.

Variations in pace, within reason, are a good way to maintain the interest and attention of the audience. It can be used to effect by, for example, using slower, more measured speech for a point that is serious or needs emphasising, or by using faster speaking to lend excitement or urgency.

The impact of the dramatic or emphasising pause should not be under-estimated. Different purposes need different lengths of pause: a comic pause to heighten a joke is ideally about three seconds; a dramatic pause, six to eight seconds. Frankly, any longer and your listeners will be looking for signs that you are still breathing.

Question 7: How loudly should I talk?

These days with all the electronic reinforcement available, this may appear to be a non-issue. But it isn't. In fact, the use of microphones can reduce the effectiveness of the use of loudness as a way to enhance a talk. It tends to compress the dynamic range that is available to a speaker, leading to an audible but rather boring talk.

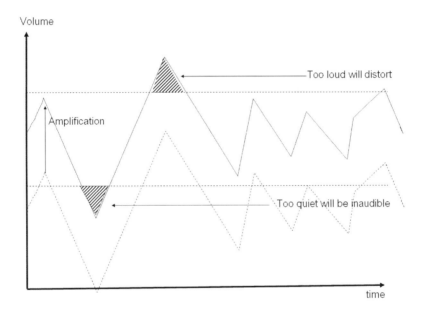

Typical modernist trick, kill off best practice in favour of improving the worst excesses up to a level of uniform mediocrity.

Let's first consider the problems that we wish to avoid.

- Speaking too quietly. Some speakers have problems generating enough volume. The solution here lies either in artificial amplification or voice training.
- Speaking too loudly. This generally is a problem where the speaker speaks too loudly for the amplification system. The solution is simple, either tone down the volume or increase the distance between the speaker and the microphone.
- Trailing off at the end of sentences. Some speakers who speak perfectly audibly for most of the sentence lose interest before the end of the sentence, and they have moved on to the next idea before finishing the sentence. The result is a

significant dip in volume leading to a loss of audibility at the end of a sentence. The speaker may be unaware of this. (I know I was!) This is one of those characteristics that you can only detect by getting a very good friend to listen to you, or by videoing yourself.

- Moving away from a static microphone. If, like me, you move around while speaking, beware the static microphone. As you move around, the distance to the microphone will vary. The volume the listeners hear will vary in inverse proportion to the distance, squared. This can be most disconcerting for them!

However, if we can avoid the common pitfalls, then variations in volume can become a useful enhancement to any talk. If possible, ditch the artificial volume stimulants. If this is not possible, then use a system which keeps microphone-to-mouth distance constant, e.g. a clip-on microphone. If this is unavailable, then take care when using a static microphone to keep a roughly constant distance.

Increased volume may be used to:

- emphasise a specific point
- build towards a climax
- introduce variation to prevent the audience falling asleep
- show enthusiasm to identify the speaker with key points in the talk.

Equally, reduced volume may be used to:

- emphasise a specific point
- engage the listeners' attention and force them to listen
- establish a degree of intimacy to connect with your listeners.

Any normal conversation has variations in speed, pitch and volume. While it is easy to caricature such variations, the reality is that without such variations, human speech quickly becomes a monotone, which is incredibly uninteresting to listen to.

Pause for thought

Try this activity to see what I mean.

- Watch a television interview with a politician to see how they use pace and volume of speaking to emphasise their points.
- Better still, listen to a radio programme where an impressionist mimics such an interview or speech. They will exaggerate these features, and they become more obvious. The lack of visual clues on the radio will focus attention on the audible rather than the visual characteristics.

Question 8: How do I reinforce my key messages without boring my listeners?

The reality is that reinforcement is key to getting a message across. However, we know that repetition can quickly become boring. Furthermore, if someone doesn't get it the first time, why would they get it the second time unless you do something different?

Therefore, the strategy of variations on a theme is a key part of any communicator's armoury. The art of variations on a theme is to repeat the same message in such a way that the listener who 'got' it the first time doesn't feel patronised or bored, and the listener who didn't get it the first time stands a chance of getting it the second time around.

I once shared an office with a very gifted teacher. A student called to see her to ask for extra help with the subject of her last lecture. They didn't get it.

So the teacher explained it a different way: they still didn't get it.

So the teacher found a third way to explain the concept: the student still didn't get it.

And a fourth . . .

And a fifth . . .

I counted ten different explanations, and still the student didn't get it. In fact, the student never did get it, but I marvelled at (a) the patience of my colleague, and (b) the way in which the same concept could be represented, 13 different ways in all.

A friend of mine who happened to call in and witness the exchange observed, 'I'm not on the course, I know nothing about the subject, but even I understood it by the end!'

This is what good communicators do: they present their information from a range of perspectives to try to maximise their chances of connecting with their listeners. We know that different people learn and absorb information in different ways, so it makes sense to seek to present your messages from a range of different perspectives.

- Some people respond to formal evidence.
- Some people respond to pragmatic illustrations.

The reality is that most groups of listeners are made of heterogeneous individuals, and their responses will also vary according to context. You may focus on their commonalities. For example:

- they all belong to a single professional group, e.g. nurses, doctors
- they all belong to a single age group, e.g. they are all younger than me, they are all older than me
- they have other things in common, e.g. gender, ethnicity, nationality

but the reality is that no group of human beings is truly homogeneous, so key messages should always be presented from a variety of perspectives if possible.

Further, reinforcement, if it can be achieved without boring the pants off the listeners, will help with retention.

To see how this might work in practice, consider the care of mental health patients. A common theme emerging from studies of the care of mental health patients is that key information is not shared. If this is a key message, it may be reinforced by considering the problem from different perspectives.

The fundamental message here is that the lack of information affects the quality of care and all the stakeholders involved with that care. Three perspectives allow us to deliver the message three times without repeating ourselves unduly.

Other types of variations on a theme include citing complementary research studies from different contexts or combining different types of evidence, e.g. a research study, an anecdote from personal experience. You can use the anecdote for insight and the evidence to demonstrate general applicability. For example:

> The bus was late last week, and I missed my outpatient's appointment. Evidence shows that the NHS in England had x000 did-not-attends due to public transport problems in 2005, at a cost of £yM.

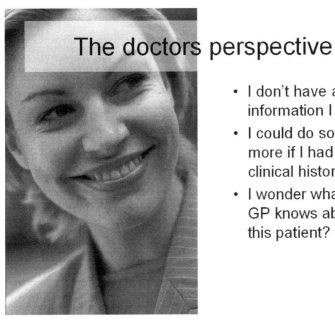

The doctors perspective

- I don't have all the information I need
- I could do so much more if I had a full clinical history
- I wonder what the GP knows about this patient?

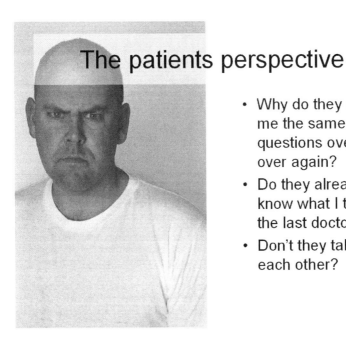

The patients perspective

- Why do they ask me the same questions over and over again?
- Do they already know what I told the last doctor?
- Don't they talk to each other?

Question 9: How do I handle questions?

If the average talk causes a physical reaction equivalent to seven cups of coffee, then answering questions must be worth at least a dozen! Questions scare people because they are the part of the process that the speaker can't control.

But there are lots of things you can do to take control of the situation.

Action	Explanation
Let the listeners know when you will take questions	If you don't want to be interrupted, then state that questions will be taken at the end
Finish your talk on time	If you don't finish your talk on time, your question slot will be truncated. While this may seem superficially attractive, it is frustrating for your listeners, and ultimately leaves you looking less than organised
Manage your time for questions	Specify how long you will allow for questions. If an answer is going to take too long, you can give a brief response then offer to discuss it later over coffee or whatever
Repeat the question back	This has two advantages. First, it ensures everyone has heard the question. Second, it gives you time to think
Beware the rambler	Ramblers can strike from the audience, too. If you meet a rambling questioner, stop them politely and ask them: 'I think your question is . . ., am I right?'
Avoid clichés and repetitious responses	Ever sat and listened to a speaker, who starts every answer with 'That's a really good question' or similar? It becomes tedious very quickly so don't do it
If you don't know, say so	Ignorance is not a crime. You can always take contact details and find out the answer. Better to keep your mouth shut and have them think you're a fool than open it and confirm it!

Following this guidance will help you achieve competence, and hopefully help you feel in control. However, questions are not just an ordeal to be overcome, they are a positive opportunity to engage with your audience and to learn from other people. So here are some things you can do to positively embrace questions.

First, allow lots of time for questions. Tell your listeners that you are doing this and why. This strategy communicates lots of really good messages. It says:

1 'I'm confident.'
2 'I value your opinion.'
3 'I believe that I don't have all the answers and can still learn from others.'

Once you have created the opportunity for a dialogue, then you need to use it constructively and maintain the initiative. Because you have created extra time for questions and dialogue, then here are a number of ways that you can make use of the opportunities provided.

Invite questions during the talk. Although this runs the risk of derailing the direction of your talk, it breaks it up, which may well help you to re-engage with those who otherwise would be starting to fall asleep. Keep control by reserving the right to curtail in-talk discussion with a line such as 'We need more time than we've got to discuss this. Let's return to it at the end.'

Invite other contributions. If you feel that your answer to a question is incomplete, then invite other views. If you are part of a panel or group of speakers, then ask them for their views. If you know that someone among your listeners has specific expertise, then ask them for a view. And don't be afraid to throw it open by asking listeners for their answers to the question posed. After all, if they say something sensible, then it adds to the discussion and you appear magnanimous, and if they spout rubbish, it makes you look good by comparison.

Plug your book or other resource that you wish to publicise. If you provide a brief response, then you can always offer the follow-up 'and you can find more information in my book/pamphlet/website/club newsletter'. This comes into the category of providing differential levels of detail for different listeners, and is discussed further in the next section.

And if you run out of time, having had a lively and positive discussion, you can always adjourn to further discussions over coffee or the poison of your choice.

Pause for thought

Are you fed up with me banging on about post-modernism? Well, in the course of researching this topic I came across the following advice (on the Web, of course), which I consider to be strictly modernist and which explains why I have maintained the distinction of the post-modernist approach:

> Be cognizant of how much time you can afford to spend answering questions. In a 60-minute talk the maximum you can afford is about five minutes. In a longer talk you can be more flexible, say 10 minutes for a 90-minute session.

I don't think this is enough. It implies that people want to listen to my voice alone for up to 80 minutes. Even I'm not that deluded about my talks.

> If you are the keynote speaker for a major conference then you should not be entertaining questions. Period.

The more important you are, the more responsibility you have to your listeners. The non-verbal (by definition) message 'I'm too important to answer questions' is particularly unpalatable. The expectation if you are an important speaker is that questions will be either non-existent or highly staged. How much more impressive, therefore, if such a speaker takes time to field genuine questions.

Still, as I said, it's good to ask for other views. What do you think?

Question 10: How much detail do I need to include in the talk?

The greatest temptation with any talk is to cram as much detail as possible into all components of a talk. In my view, a talk may have up to five components:

- pre-reading
- handouts
- presentation graphics
- the talk itself
- follow-up activities.

Very often, we simply duplicate what we seek to do with each component. Where is the sense in that? Reinforcement, you may say. Well, there's reinforcement and there's doing something to death! Here's my presentation on doing a talk to death.

Doing a talk to death

- This is characterised by pre-reading that actually covers everything in the talk –

In that case, why bother turning up?

Doing a talk to death

- The talk itself is accompanied by hand-outs that simply reproduce every word of the talk –

In that case, why bother listening to the talk?

Doing a talk to death

• The slides are simply the script chopped up and put onto either acetate or presentation slides –

Far too much information to read or take in.

Doing a talk to death

• The talk itself has already been given to the listeners in the handouts and can be read off the slides –

Why bother to talk?

Doing a talk to death

• I don't think your listeners would follow up –

Why would they?

Those that have not given up will have found out everything anyway.

If this seems like a caricature, then it is, right down to the grim reaper, but some real-life experiences have got pretty close to it.

Instead of this blanket approach, why not try to find complementary roles for each component? Consider the analysis in the table below.

Imagine each component in the talk as a member of the team. You would not ask every team member to do everything. You would divide up the tasks you wish to achieve among the team, hopefully according to each team member's strengths.

So in thinking about your talk, divide up the goals of the talk among the components of the talk, according to their strengths and weaknesses, and do not seek to get them all doing the same thing five times over!

Component	Strengths	How you might use it
Pre-reading	Can draw on a range of sources Can draw on significant detail Can be ignored by the listener if not relevant to them	To bring all your listeners up to a common level of initial knowledge, and make the talk relevant to a varied group of listeners To communicate background information To engage your listeners' interest in your topic
Handouts	Can draw on a range of sources Can draw on significant detail A permanent resource, that can be taken away Can be ignored by the listener if not relevant to them	To provide detailed information To provide supporting case studies, examples and evidence To provide copies of your slides with space for listeners to make notes To provide information to meet different prior knowledge levels and needs of readers
Graphics	Can be used alongside the talk to complement the talk itself Can form part of the hand-out	To reinforce points from the talk To structure the talk To punctuate the talk
The talk itself	It is the interactive component It can be flexible and varied	To enthuse the listeners To explain complex concepts, perhaps from multiple perspectives To emphasise key points To lead up to the take-home message To respond to the listeners' needs and reactions
Follow-up activities	Can be open-ended Are owned by the listeners Can be referred to in response to questions	To encourage the listeners to find out more To encourage the listeners to do something (differently) as a result of the talk To answer a question in more detail than otherwise possible

4 Ten things to do with presentation graphics that aren't bulleted lists that whizz in and do a quick orbit before settling down in a font that can't be read from the front row

Things to do 1: Go minimal

You will be unsurprised to learn that, as an information management professional, I do still use presentation graphics software. However, over the years I have developed a series of strategies to try to ensure that the presentation graphics enhance the talk. The first approach is strictly modernist and is governed by the guidance provided in Chapter 3.

The guiding principle here is minimalism. So the design template is almost black and white with just the university logo to provide some colour. The black text on white background maximises the contrast, and a simple Arial font guarantees a consistent look wherever the presentation is shown.

This style of presentation is not designed to be viewed on its own. Each point may be expounded in the talk and expanded on. So, for example, the point

Use a mixture of upper and lower case

could be expounded as:

Using a mixture of upper and lower case provides better clarity than simply upper case or lower case on its own. Think about the lettering on motorway signs. Previously, road signs used upper case only, but the use of a clear type face known as Transport and a mixture of cases provides much greater clarity.

So does this presentation follow all its own 'rules'? Pretty much.

- There are no more than five points per slide.
- Each point is short, although some have more than six words; but surely in a post-modern world, six is an aspiration.
- If this talk was planned at more than 10 minutes, then five slides is OK.
- There is only one font.
- As there is only one font, it cannot mix serif and sans serif, although the use of sans serif fits with the university logo.
- It does use a mixture of upper and lower case.
- There are no diagrams.
- It avoids bright colours, complex backgrounds and whizzy transitions.

So you think this is minimalist? Well, it could be more minimalist. You don't have to use a set of slides at all. You could just talk. There are situations where the slides just distract.

Or you could use a slide show like this to structure your thoughts beforehand, but not when you are talking.

Or you could use a slide show like this to structure your talk by generating hand-outs for listeners to make notes while you are talking. In this case, you can use the slides as prompts.

The trick is not to get ideological about minimalism. It is not a good thing per se. But it is a means to put the talking back where it belongs: centre stage. It is a way of challenging the orthodoxy that more is better, and that the technology in some way replaces the talking or negates the need to get the talking right.

Less is more: guidance

- Never put more than 5 points on one slide
- Keep each point short
- Don't have >1 slide per 2 minutes talking
- Don't use more than two fonts,
- Don't mix serif and san serif fonts

Email: talking@alangillies.com

Less is more: guidance

- Use a mixture of upper and lower case
- Keep diagrams simple
- Avoid bright colours
- Avoid busy backgrounds
- Don't have too many whizzy transitions

Email: talking@alangillies.com

Features of this style

- High clarity
- Simplicity
- Provides a basis for verbal exposition
- Dull on its own
- Repetitive for longer presentation

Email: talking@alangillies.com uclan

A short guide to keeping things simple

Professor Alan Gillies

Email: talking@alangillies.com uclan

Less is more

- Many presentations are too complex
- Many talks are too long
- Minimalism can focus attention on key points
- High contrast ensures visibility
- Fewer points makes slides simpler
- Fewer slides makes talks fit their slot

Email: talking@alangillies.com uclan

Less is more: guidance

- Never put more than 5 points on one slide
- Keep each point short
- Don't have >1 slide per 2 minutes talking
- Don't use more than two fonts,
- Don't mix serif and san serif fonts

Email: talking@alangillies.com uclan

Things to do 2: Use the graphics before and after but not during

The impact of presentation graphics is usually diminished by repetition (see later for an honourable exception). An alternative take on the minimalist approach is to use a graphic to set up a question at the beginning of a talk and one at the end to reinforce the take-home message, with unsupported talking in between.

It's a technique that I have used successfully in a job interview, but it may lend itself to other contexts as well. It is suited to situations where you have one key theme, text or question around which the whole talk is based. The graphics become bookends framing the talk and acting to reinforce the initial statement, question or text at the beginning and reinforcing your conclusion at the end, but not distracting from the spoken word in the middle. Further information can be supplied as hand-outs.

Consider, for example, the following question: can a computer improve my life? To which we might pose the answer: yes, but only if:

- you have a problem amenable to computerisation
- you have the right skills to use it
- you have the right application
- you have the right data to input into the computer.

Each of these would be a theme in the talk itself, but could be expounded verbally with the use of examples and evidence from a range of situations.

The sparse use of the supporting graphic increases its effectiveness in reinforcing the key theme and conclusions.

Your bookend slides might look like this:

Things to do 3: Fluffy clouds

Supposing that you really really want to use a bulleted list. It's not a crime, we used them in our minimalist presentation. But they can get:

- dull
- repetitive
- boring
- and so on

if they are repeated slide after slide.

Attempts to jazz them up by making them whizz in and do a quick orbit before settling down are often counterproductive, so here's my post-modern alternative, the fluffy cloud approach:

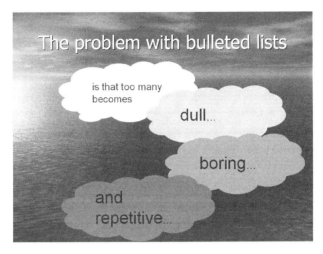

This version is produced on a single slide in the following steps.

- In Microsoft PowerPoint, open a new show and adopt the ocean template (stored as ocean.pot).
- Enter the title as shown.
- Delete the main text box.
- From the Autoshapes menu select 'Callouts' and then the 'thinks bubble'.
- Draw the callout for the first cloud.
- To make the first cloud, set fill and line properties to white, then tuck the tail up inside the cloud so it disappears.
- Add a text box, type your text and set the text colour to blue and outline colour to white.
- Change the font to Arial.
- Group the text and shape.
- Copy the group.
- Paste a new cloud.
- Edit the text, and set the graphic colours to a light shade of grey.
- Repeat for each cloud, setting progressively darker shades of grey.
- Finally, set the entrance transition to appear for each cloud.

Remember, less is more. If you use this for every slide, it's just another boring bulleted list. Use it occasionally to break up the routine.

And in case the clouds and ocean thing is too much here's a more modernistic version based on the minimalist style.

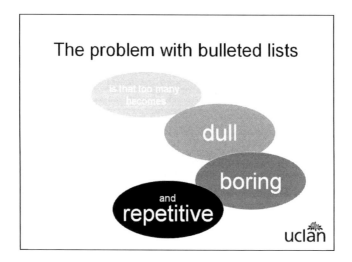

Things to do 4: Build transition: explaining a process

One of my biggest pet hates from the pre-modernist era of public speaking was the users of overheads who manually used to cover up the lower portions to reveal the points one by one. It drove me mad for several reasons:

- it is very difficult to do competently
- consequently, it was very rarely done competently and bits of paper often ended up all over the floor.

It generally left me feeling frustrated, distracted and rather patronised.

The modernist equivalent is the bulleted list that builds point by point. It's much slicker than the old paper-based process, but it's still frustratingly controlling by the speaker. It can lead to a rather staccato style of presentation where the flow is destroyed by waiting for the next point to appear. It is worth remembering that while a talk has distinct phases and chunks, it is essentially designed to flow. Therefore a series of bulleted lists with each point waiting to be clicked is essentially at odds with a talk, which should flow.

However, there are situations where this fragmentation can be used to advantage. In a situation where the task is to break up a process into its constituent parts, then this becomes an advantage. Consider for example a slide intended to show the nature of the clinical audit cycle, which I used recently. By breaking down the process into its constituent parts, the slide can actually reinforce the key message that the total waiting time is made up of a number of components, as in the example shown.

This slide was produced in Microsoft PowerPoint using the drawing tool bar to good effect.

- The arrows were chosen from the Autoshapes menu.
- They were chosen from the Block arrows category.
- A 3D effect is then added, and colours to taste.

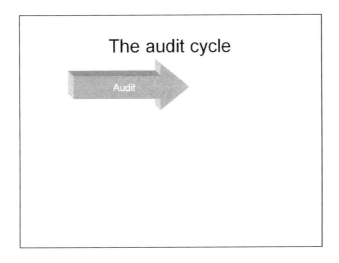

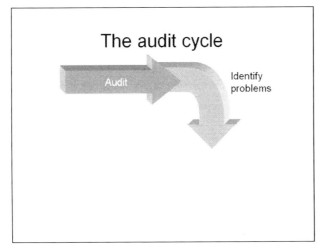

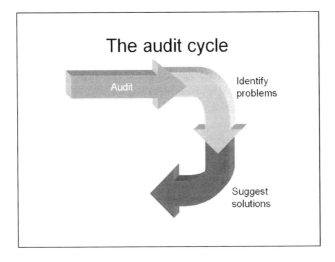

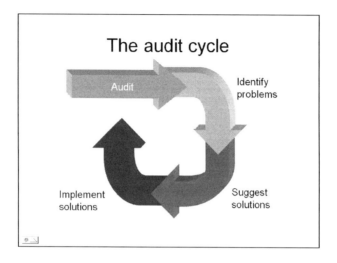

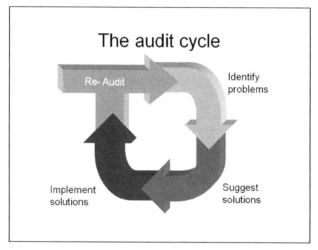

Things to do 5: Images for reinforcement

Images provide a great opportunity to emphasise or reinforce a key message. They only work if used sparingly. One per key message is a good guide – if you have too many images and they are losing their impact, then the answer is to cram fewer key messages in there. Less is more!

I suggest that there are at least three ways to use an image for reinforcement. The first is to use positive reinforcement, an image designed to support the message that is being communicated. For example:

Using a computer should be child's play!

The key message here is 'Using a computer should be child's play'.

While the image has cuteness on its side, it is a sad fact that in our cynical world, negative reinforcement can be more powerful by using a negative image to emphasise the consequences of not following a key message. Consider the following two examples, negatively reinforcing the key messages:

- using a computer should be child's play (but too often, it isn't)
- talks need to hold the audience's attention (but this one didn't!).

Using a computer should be child's play (but too often, it isn't)

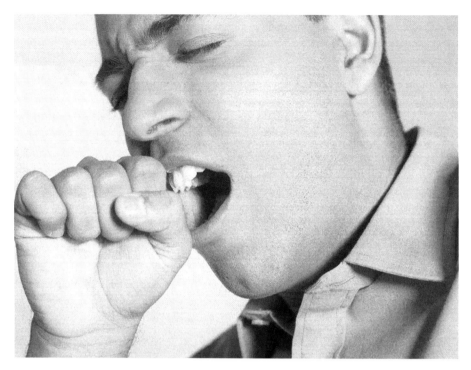

Talks need to hold the audience's attention (but this one didn't!)

Humorous images can be used, but all the usual caveats about using humour apply.

It is also important to respect copyright. All the images used in this book have been purchased under a royalty-free licensing arrangement. Just because you find an image or cartoon on the Web, it doesn't mean it's free to use. Very often, if you are in a non-profit-making situation you can gain permission to use an image, but you should always ask the copyright owner first. 🐾

One of the commonest ways that speakers use images to emphasise key points is through the use of graphs to summarise numerical data. This can be very useful because:

- many listeners don't like numbers
- many listeners like pictures
- graphs can reduce large amounts of data to a much simpler representation
- computers provide very convenient ways to draw very attractive graphs.

🐾 The images provided in this book are either my own or downloaded under licence from a commercial supplier. As such, I have permission to use them within my own book, on my website and in my own presentations. If you email me, I can provide those presentations. However, it would be a breach of copyright for you to extract those images from the presentations and use them for another purpose. I can tell you how to acquire them legally for another purpose. YOU HAVE BEEN WARNED!

However, as always, there are some pitfalls.

The first is that screen after screen of charts in the same format is very tedious. The impact is lost. If you wish to communicate detailed results or numbers using lots of charts, then make up a hand-out and distribute it or offer it to your listeners at the end to follow up the detail.

The reality is that not all findings hold the same interest. Some are more interesting than others – these are your key messages and should be highlighted in your talk with a chart.

The second pitfall is that there are certain types of chart that are not a good idea. Here are three very attractive charts that each have at least one major gaffe. They are the sort of thing that you might produce in a spreadsheet package and then copy and paste onto a presentation slide. And they are all based on examples I've actually seen! Try and spot the gaffes before you proceed. If you want to find out more about this topic, try reading Anna Hart's book (details in the Further reading section).

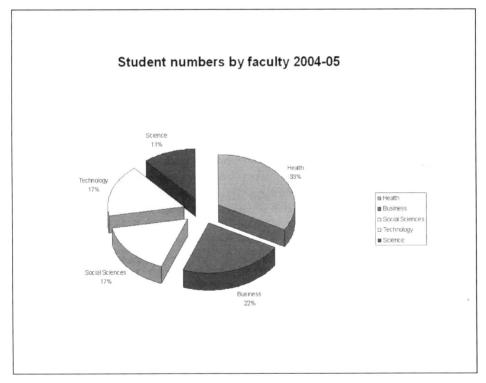

Chart 1

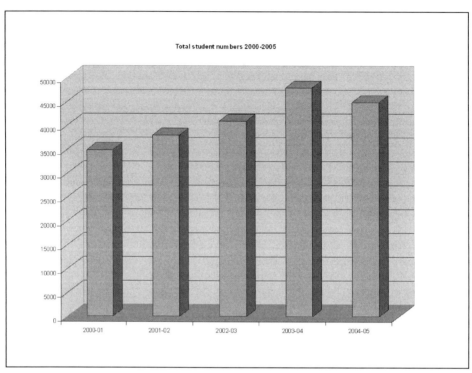

Chart 2

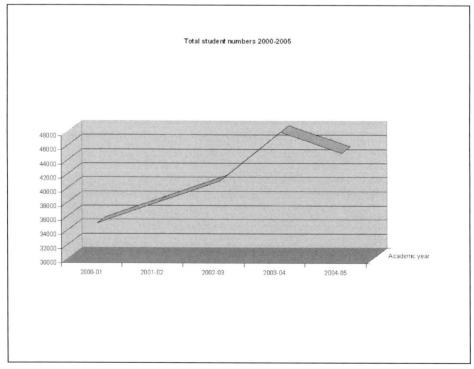

Chart 3

So what's wrong with chart 1?

Pie charts are not a very good idea at all. There is research evidence to show that we find it difficult to perceive proportion when displayed around a circle. In this case, splitting up the pie, making it three-dimensional and adding a 45 degree viewing angle renders it almost impossible.

To these problems, we may add font sizes generated automatically by the computer within the spreadsheet that become far too small when copied and pasted onto the slide.

So what's wrong with chart 2?

Spreadsheet graphics applications have encouraged us to use three-dimensional charts. In a bar chart, it simply adds a degree of uncertainty as to where the top of the bar actually is. The background adds to the uncertainty, as do the gaps between the bars. Add to this the problems of the previous chart in terms of inappropriate font sizes generated automatically, and the result may be best described as 'suboptimal'.

So what's wrong with chart 3?

In addition to the problems raised with charts 1 and 2, which this chart shares, we may add two further problems. One is the use of a false origin at 30,000, which exaggerates the differences, and the second is the plotting of a trend based on discrete data. Students do not join the university continuously but at the start of a year, or in a few cases, a semester, therefore plotting a trend is misleading. Have a look at the two versions that follow, the first is a more satisfactory version of chart 1, the second of charts 2 and 3.

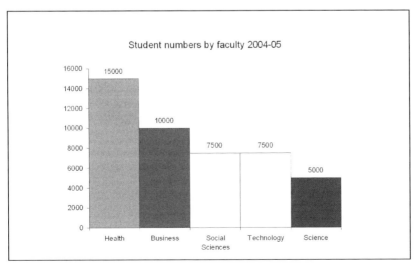

Chart 1 revisited

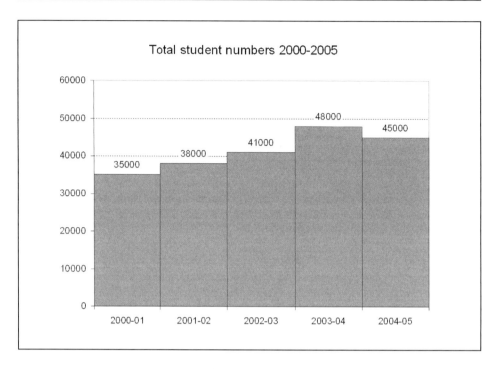

Chart 2/3 revisited

 **Pause for thought**

It's not just amateur or even professional speakers who abuse graphs and charts. Reputable media organisations do it all the time.

Try visiting the BBC website or those of national newspapers and look at how they represent data. I'll be amazed if you can't find false origins and pie charts at the very least!

Things to do 6: Take a tiered approach to detail

A talk is made up of a collection of elements as we have already seen. Therefore we can use different levels of detail in different elements.

As a listener, we may wish to engage with different levels of detail for different purposes. As a speaker, we should facilitate people accessing different levels of detail.

If we consider an onion structure of differential detail, then we may end up with something like this:

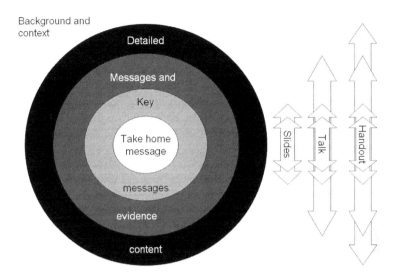

At the heart of our talk is the key take-home message. This should be evident in all elements of our talk. Key messages should also be present in all elements.

Most presentation graphics seek to encompass not just the key messages, but also the evidence to support them. Very often this leads to clutter and overload. In this model, it is suggested that this is not the role of the presentation graphics: instead, there should be less content in the presentation graphics and more emphasis on ramming home the key messages through reinforcement.

The Web is a great resource, but broken links are a hazard.

More detailed content can be provided in the talk itself. If a permanent record is required, then a hand-out may be provided. In general, the talk should contain more detail than the slides. The hand-out can provide more detailed information. Background information can be referred to as further reading. In this day and age, very often a list of Web URLs can provide quick and easy access to a wealth of additional information, but remember to check any links, as they can break at any time.

Things to do 7: Use presentation slides as milestones or signposts

Very often people tell me that they use presentation graphics to structure a talk. This is a laudable aim: people like to know where they are, and where they are up to. However, if you use slides for content as well, it can be confusing. If you use the talk and a hand-out to convey the content, then the slides can be left just to provide milestones along the way.

I once used the milestones image literally in a talk based around the history of computing in primary healthcare. The talk was divided into four historical phases, and when we reached the end of one and the start of the next I literally used a milestone to indicate that we had entered the next phase:

Primary care computing : a history

- Pre history pre 1990
- 1990-1997: The growth spurt
- 1997-2004: We need to join things up!
- 2004: To GMS and beyond

 uclan

Stage I: pre history (initiation)

- Adopted by enthusiasts
- Rapid change and development
- Not regarded as core by majority

uclan

1990: a milestone

- The 1990 GP contract

uclan

1997-8: a milestone or two

- A new Government
- The New NHS
- Information for health

uclan

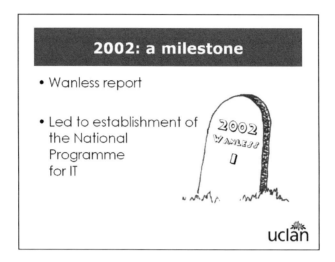

If you feel slightly less courageous, then you may like to consider signposting a less sparse presentation to reassure the user that they know where they are. The modernist approach is to use a slide X of Y message in the footer. I have three problems with this:

- It doesn't tell you where you are – just how far you are from your destination.
- It reinforces the subliminal message that the talk is the slides.
- It promotes the view that the purpose of the talk is to get to the end, not to enjoy the journey. If this is the case, why bother giving the talk at all? After all, the quickest way to get to the end of the talk is not to give it.

We have all sat through talks where the thing we want to know is how much longer is there to go, but if you are the speaker, then this is not what you want your listeners to be thinking.

Consider the following examples of slides which illustrate the difference between signposting where you are and how far you are from the destination. Note that the second example doesn't leave the listener guessing where you are up to, but provides an estimate of progress: 1, 2, 3 blobs out of 6. Notice also that the footer on the first slide is in a small font and possibly impossible to read.

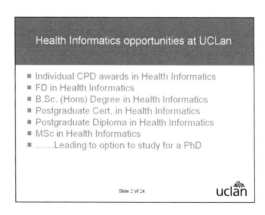

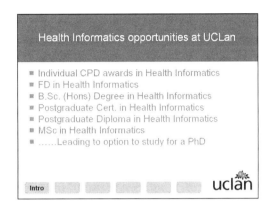

Do you want to know how far to go, or where you are?

Things to do 8: Repetition for reinforcement

In general, we have been fairly negative about repetition in this book. However, there are situations where repetition is used to reinforce a key point. Remember the Prime Minister's message of 'Education, Education, Education' in 1997? Consider the following example based on the 'rules' in Chapter 3.

Here are two versions of the same presentation.

Version 1: Emphasises individual points

This presentation provides a slide for each rule or warning. There is a strong visual theme running through the presentation, achieved through the use of traffic warning signs, both real and contrived. The use of warning signs based on red triangles rather than red circles, indicating prohibition and rules, sends a strong non-verbal signal that these are warnings for guidance rather than hard-and-fast rules. Sharp-eyed readers of previous titles of mine will have seen different versions of this, but being essentially modernist, they emphasised rules rather than warnings. This version is much more post-modernist with its strong message of warning, rather than prohibition. It uses repetition to emphasise a single, core message, that less is more, and presents all nine specific points as examples of one single rule. This is likely to leave listeners with a strong single message that they will remember.

It places less emphasis on individual aspects and more on the principle. It is less prescriptive than the one that follows. Suppose you agree with the principle that points should be kept short, but think six words are just too few. (I do!)

Hopefully there is enough variation on each slide to stop the repeated title becoming a problem. The use of one slide that bucks the trend (More is more!) is designed to actually emphasise the norm and to show that within the paradigm of this book, very little of the guidance offered is actually universal.

Warning 1:
Don't put more than
five points on one slide

5 lines

- If you find yourself in danger of ignoring this warning, best practice is to say less and remove some text
- If not, make two slides

Warning 2:
Keep each point short

- Use no more than 6 words per point
- If you find yourself in danger of ignoring this warning, best practice is to say less and remove some text
- If not, make two slides

Warning 3:
Don't have too many slides

- **not more than 1 slide per 2 minutes talking (120 seconds)**
- If you find yourself in danger of ignoring this warning, best practice is to say less and remove a slide or two

Warning 4:
Don't use more than two fonts,
and don't mix serif and san serif fonts

- Times New Roman is an example of a serif font,
- Arial is an example of a san serif font

Too many fonts

Warning 5:
Do not use all the same case

- it's easier to read a mixture of upper and lower case
- Look at the slides on the next page to decide which is the easiest to read

Warning 6:
Complex diagrams are illegible

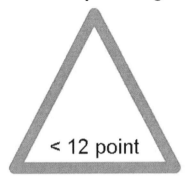

They often include text which is too small in upper or lower case, and are offered with the feeble excuse "I know you can't read this at the back"

Warning 7: Avoid bright colours

Subtlety is a virtue. (Not always encouraged by PowerPoint et al!)

Avoid bright colours, especially in large amounts as they can be distracting, tiring and irritating to viewers

Warning 8: Avoid busy backgrounds

- **Complex patterns can seem like a good idea but can be extremely harmful!**
- At best they can distracting and at worst they can completely obliterate the message. If you don't like a flat background why not use a graded background?

Warning 9:
Don't have too many whizzy transitions

- Animation is great fun but too much can weary very quickly.

Version 2: Emphasises a unifying theme

In this alternative version, there is more emphasis on individual warnings. It retains the unifying visual theme, but each slide has its own header.

This version may be rejected as too prescriptive, while the first may be more acceptable and still encourage listeners to keep their points concise.

Judge for yourself!

**Warning 1:
Less is more!**

- **Never put more than five points on one slide**
- If you find yourself in danger of ignoring this warning, best practice is to say less and remove some text
- If not, make two slides

5 lines

Warning 2:
Less is more! (again)

- **Keep each point short, use no more than 6 words per point**
- If you find yourself in danger of ignoring this warning, best practice is to say less and remove some text
- If not, make two slides

Warning 3:
Less is more! (again)

- **Don't have too many slides, not more than 1 slide per 2 minutes talking (120 seconds)**
- If you find yourself in danger of ignoring this warning, best practice is to say less and remove a slide or two

Warning 4:
Less is more! (again)

Too many fonts

- **Don't use more than two fonts, and don't mix serif and san serif fonts**
- Times New Roman is an example of a serif font, Arial is an example of a san serif font

Warning 5: More is more!

Fog

- **Do not use all the same case, as it's easier to read a mixture of upper and lower case**
- Just for once, more is more, more cases, upper AND lower is more readable

Warning 6:
Less is more! (again)

Complex diagrams are illegible. They often include text which is too small in upper or lower case, and are offered with the feeble excuse "I know you can't read this at the back"

Warning 7:
Less is more! (again)

Avoid bright colours

Subtlety is a virtue. (Not always encouraged by PowerPoint et al!) Avoid bright colours, especially in large amounts as they can be distracting, tiring and irritating to viewers

Warning 8:Less is more! (again)

- **Complex patterns can seem like a good idea but can be extremely harmful!**
- At best they can distracting and at worst they can completely obliterate the message. If you don't like a flat background why not use a graded background?

Warning 9: Less is more! (again)

Don't have too many whizzy transitions

Animation is great fun but too much can weary very quickly.

Things to do 9: Send on the warm-up act

In the entertainment business, the idea of the warm-up act is a long and honourable tradition. In the more formal academic arena, we have long encouraged the idea of pre-reading. But how many times do you actually do it?

If you like the idea of using graphics to communicate and reinforce your message, then how about separating it from your talk and letting it run beforehand as a warm-up act? Of course, this may not always be possible but where it is, it can be powerful as well as keeping the punters entertained until the main feature.

Consider, for example, the following as a warm-up act to a talk about the computerisation of general practice.

Watford Gap Motorway Services was the first in the UK.
It was also the site of England's first
GP Computing exhibition in 1983

However, in the 1980s, GP computing remained a
minority sport for most GPs

Some of the early technology was difficult to use

But in the 1990 contract came incentives to use
the new technology

By 1998, over 98% of practices had computers

And after the GMS contract of 2004, over 98% were actually using them

This provides some history, exactly the kind of thing that you would expect in pre-reading.

The presentation itself is designed to look more like a cinematic presentation than a traditional presentation, with large images and few words to maximise impact. It could be set to present on a pre-timed loop. I tried a 10-second delay between images and a simple fade through black transition between pages.

Obviously, in a real situation, you may like to use more pages, which would run for longer before the pages are repeated. However, the more pages you use, the more you dilute the key messages.

Back to your primary purpose. Is it to keep them entertained until you start, or to communicate key messages? You can do both, but there is a trade-off at some point.

Having used this kind of approach in the warm-up, a simple presentation would support, not detract from, your talk.

Things to do 10: Clues for non-native speakers

So what about the good old-fashioned set of bulleted lists? Do they have a place? If they are so bad, why did they become so popular in the first place?

Bulleted lists offer a lowest common denominator approach: they provide structure, and provided they are not overloaded, they can help the listener to follow your talk. One environment in which they can be extremely helpful is a bilingual situation. I attended a bilingual conference in Quebec. The English speakers spoke English; the French speakers spoke French, and the Québecois spoke Québecois. My French is limited and does not extend to the differences between French and Québecois, although I am convinced that France and Quebec can claim alongside the US and UK to be two races divided by a common language.

I sat through a presentation in French and would not have been able to follow the presentation without the simple slides of bulleted lists that accompanied the talk, even though they also were in French. They provided me with a summary of the sense of the talk, the key points, at a pace that even my rudimentary French could absorb. Being written, not spoken, they were also largely free of the dialect of the speaker.

I have been invited to present in France. My hosts have assured me that the audience will understand my English and are too courteous to point out that they may not be able to understand my French! So in this case, I plan to use largely simple bulleted lists as an accompaniment to my talk and to have them translated into French.

I shall talk in my own language . . . I understand your language but will understand more with the help of summary points . . . and more still with a summary in my own language.

5 The take-home message

So, what is the take-home message from this book? It's tough to pull out a single take-home message from a whole book, but if there is one key message, it is that:

> presentation graphics are there to support the talk and not the other way around

The whole point of the book is to re-establish the principle that the most important part of any talk is the spoken word and all the other bits are there to support that. Within this view, you can use different elements (pre-reading, presentation graphics, hand-outs and post-reading) for different but complementary purposes.

This will avoid my two pet hates: slide after slide of bulleted lists attempting to provide a detailed script for the whole talk read out by the speaker, or alternatively a whizz-bang presentation that renders the talk itself an irrelevant sideshow.

A secondary theme is 'less is more': fewer slides, fewer points, shorter points, fewer fonts, simpler backgrounds, fewer bright colours and fewer whizzy transitions. In order to achieve this, I commend to you the approach based on complementary use of the different components as outlined at the end of Chapter 4.

So, to explore your view of this take-home message, consider whether you accept the following 10 propositions offered through the book in its support.

 **Pause for thought**

How many of the following propositions do you agree with:

1 Most of the talks I have listened to recently have not excited or inspired me.
2 Where this was true, the supporting presentation graphics were no more engaging than the talk itself.
3 In many cases, I do not recall the detail of the talk.

4 There were too many slides containing too much information.
5 Images used did not help me to remember key points.
6 I would welcome talks that engage me.
7 I would like to remember the key points from talks I was interested in.
8 Talks I remember well used presentation graphics in a distinctive fashion.
9 Good speakers handle questions well.
10 A good talk inspires one to find out more about the subject afterwards.

So how many of my propositions do you agree with?

Propositions agreed with	What I think
9–10	I hope you enjoyed reading the book. You certainly seem sympathetic to its key message
5–8	My sort of reader. You obviously sympathise with most of the book, but think for yourself. So go out and do talks that reflect that thoughtful individuality!
2–4	I apologise for wasting your time. But why are you still reading?
0–1	You haven't really read it, have you? You just skipped to the end to read the take-home message. Otherwise you'd have given up on me long ago. Possibly, you wouldn't enjoy one of my talks either!

6 The afterword

Why is there an afterword? The book clearly states that the take-home message comes at the end, but here is an afterword. The book also recognises that a component of any talk is what the listeners do afterwards.

The book is a talk, it's written not spoken, but it has been conceived as a talk. The talk finished with the take-home message in Chapter 6. The afterword is therefore about what you do after this 'talk'. All the way through I have tried to use the devices that I have advocated to aid communication. See, for example, how the section on handling questions ends on a question.

The first possible action is nothing. Just close the book. Dig out your corporate templates and go back to reading through your bulleted lists and calling it a 'talk'. Hopefully, however, you may want to do more. Here are three things you may like to do.

1　Think about the book as a talk. Think about the advice I have given. Use the checklist to evaluate not just the sample slides but the text of the book as well. It's not just about ticking the boxes: where the book departs from the guidance there may be a good reason.
2　Think about recent talks you have given. Use the checklist to evaluate not just the slides you used but the words spoken and any hand-outs as well. It's not just about conforming to the views in this book, you may have had good reasons for departing from the guidance given here, the question to think about is, if you do depart from the guidance is there a justifiable reason?
3　Email me with feedback requests for copies of any slides or other materials in the book, or with a willingness to join an online community to discuss the issues raised in the book.

Planning	Yes	No
Is there a clear aim for the talk?		
Is there a clear take-home message?		
Are the other key messages obvious?		
Is the level of assumed prior knowledge correct?		
Is the planned length appropriate for the content delivered?		
Delivery		
Was the pace about right?		
Was the delivered length according to plan?		
Were there too many rambling anecdotes in the text?		
Did the humour grate on you? (What humour? See what I mean?)		
Did the delivery keep your attention?		
Slides		
Do the slides add to the talk?		
Do the slides have a distinct purpose?		
Are there too many points on any slides?		
Are the individual points kept short?		
Are there no more than two fonts, and only serif or sans serif fonts?		
Are the diagrams simple?		
Are the charts simple and unambiguous?		
Do the images used reinforce or distract from key messages?		
Hand-outs		
Are there hand-outs or other supporting materials?		
Do they add to the talk?		
Do they have a distinct purpose?		
Do they contain or point to information beyond what is in the talk?		

The Appendix: the handouts

At the end of Chapter 3, I argued that a talk was not simply a talk, but a collection of entities that could be thought of as a team, and that we should allocate the intended objectives for the talk to the appropriate team member:

1 Pre-reading
2 Handouts
3 Graphics
4 The talk itself
5 Follow-up activities.

By now, you will have seen that the book has been designed as a talk, and the talk is intended to embody the advice contained within its pages as far as possible. Therefore, this section is not part of the talk itself, but rather the handouts to accompany the talk. Its purpose is to provide more detail or information that would distract from the main talk if included in the talk, or simply make the talk too long.

Handout 1: The completed plan for the book

Issue	Answer for this book
What is the aim of the talk?	The aim is to try to help people make their public talks more interesting and effective. The benefits were intended to be for the listeners as much as the speakers.
	Finally, the book was intended to show that the epidemic of boring talks accompanied by long tedious collections of bulleted lists are not the fault of the computers or even of the developers of PowerPoint, but are due to the failure of speakers to use these tools in a way that actually enhances their talks.
What are your objectives?	The objectives are:
	1 To establish the proposition that the almost ubiquitous use of electronic presentation graphics to accompany public speaking is sub-optimal, and many times does not enhance, or actually detracts from, the spoken word.
	2 To show how effective planning can enhance public speaking and enable you to tailor your talk to the context in which it is delivered.
	3 To provide advice on how to improve public speaking and to challenge some of the orthodox advice which promotes the view that there is one single way to do it right.
	4 To show how technology can be used to enhance a talk and to encourage speakers to be more flexible in their use of technology, emphasising the primacy of the spoken word.
Who is the target audience?	The target audience is those engaged in public speaking, not necessarily with the aid of technology. This includes, but is not limited to:
	• College and University lecturers tired of giving the same old talk with the same old bulleted lists.
	• Experienced public speakers who have discovered that slide projectors are much harder to get hold of, and want to find new ways of delivering their talk.
	• Workers from the public or private sector who want to share knowledge with colleagues but remember falling asleep at the last event they attended and want to avoid having the same effect.
	• Preachers and worship leaders in our churches who have just discovered information technology and want to be seen to be up to date and relevant to younger people.
What knowledge may be assumed?	A basic experience of public speaking is assumed.
	In order to implement many of the ideas about the creative use of information technology, a basic knowledge of a presentation graphics package and a more limited knowledge of a word processing package are assumed.
	Where this is lacking, it may be gained by reading *Presenting Health with PowerPoint* as a pre-reading activity.
	The Flesch Reading Ease score is 61.3, and the Flesch-Kincaid Grade Level score is 8.4, which indicates a text which should be comprehensible to an average 13-year-old. A glossary is provided as a handout to help with comprehension.

Issue	Answer for this book
How long should it be?	Books have a minimum sensible length otherwise they run the risk of being called 'pamphlets' by students (it happened to me) and 'uneconomic' by publishers. This is generally around 120–130 pages.
	The length here is intended to be the minimum required to convey the messages that it is designed to convey. It's on the short side as books go, but you didn't want me to waffle on, did you?
How many sections/ chunks of knowledge should there be?	There are three main sections to the book, each divided into 10 subsections, together with an introduction and a concluding section in three parts with the handouts appended at the end.
What are the key messages?	The key messages of this book are:
	1 I have been to too many talks which were frankly boring.
	2 I have seen too many talks ruined by repetitive bulleted lists used as presentation graphics.
	3 Planning is important for any talk, the more spontaneous you wish to appear, the better planned you need to be.
	4 Context is everything.
	5 You can use technology in a wide variety of ways to enhance the spoken word.
	6 The talk is a collection of components, including pre-reading, handouts and presentation graphics as well as the spoken word: use the best component for the job.
What is the take-home message?	The take-home message is:
	'Presentation graphics are there to support the talk and not the other way round'.
What do you expect your listeners to do with the talk?	The book will have worked if it inspires public speakers to:
	1 Re-evaluate their own public speaking.
	2 Encourage them to plan more effectively.
	3 Consider the audience and context for their talk.
	4 Use technology in a more varied and effective way.
	5 Use handouts and pre-reading more effectively.
	6 Communicate more effectively with their listeners.

Handout 2: The division of labour

Component	What was done	The purpose
Pre-reading	The principal pre-reading for this book is: Gillies AC. *Presenting Health with PowerPoint*. Oxford: Radcliffe Publishing; 2003 for those readers whose knowledge of the technology was below the standard assumed.	This was done because it would have been inappropriate to include detailed information about how to use technology in a book whose central message was that the blind use of technology has devalued the worth of the spoken word. Secondly, many of the target readers would already have the required level of knowledge in this area.
Handouts	The handouts are where you are now. They include sections to show the book itself was planned using the techniques espoused within its pages, as well as a glossary and information about further resources.	If included in the main text, this material would have detracted from the clarity of the messages to be communicated. In particular, it seemed useful to separate material about how the book was constructed from the book content in order to prevent the whole thing disappearing up its own navel!
Graphics	Graphics are included in the main text.	The graphics are used for the purposes argued for in the main text: • reinforcement • explanation • humour • as milestones.
The talk itself	The talk is the main content of the book. The writing style is intended to speak to the reader as spoken word rather than a more formal style generally associated with the written word.	If the book is to have impact, then it must have credibility and the author must be seen to be competent and to practice what he preaches. The written text has the dual purpose of communicating the messages and demonstrating their use and credibility. It is of course for the reader to decide whether this goal is achieved!
Follow-up activities	The book encourages the reader to go away and apply the messages from the book for themselves.	The success of the book will be measured by the number of readers who change their practice as a consequence of reading the book. Strictly, it should be measured by the number of listeners who think that this change is for the better!

Handout 3: The glossary

The glossary is intended to not just explain terms used, but to indicate the particular way in which the author has used the terms, and also to cover some of those pesky abbreviations.

Think of the safety announcements at the start of a flight:

> We request your attention for the following safety announcement. Even if you are a frequent flyer, please pay attention because each plane is different and your safety is our priority.

To paraphrase:

> I request your attention for the following glossary of terms. Even if you are a very clever person who thinks you understand all the terms used in this book, please pay attention because each author is different and your comprehension is our priority.

Term/abbreviation	Meaning
AA	The abbreviation can refer to the 'Automobile Association' or 'Alcoholics Anonymous'. Important one to get right!
AI	AI usually means 'artificial intelligence' to the IT community, but 'artificial insemination' to the medical community.
BBC	It used to mean the British Broadcasting Corporation, who aside from making excellent television programmes have an increasing presence on the World Wide Web, and are providing many useful resources for presenters for non-commercial use.
BSc	BSc stands for Batchelor of Science: it features on some of my slides.
DNA	Could be 'Did not attend' or alternatively '**deoxyribonucleic** acid'. 'Did not attend' is easier to say.
FdSc	FdSc stands for Foundation Degree in Science: it features on some of my slides.
Font	In computing terms, the word font is used synomynously with 'typeface'. The world is divided into serif fonts like Times New Roman and sans serif fonts like Arial.
GPs/GPS	GPs will mean 'general practitioners' to the medical community, but 'Geographical Positioning Systems' to the IT community. Case of the letters may be key here, but in a verbal presentation or under the influence of computerised auto-correction facilities, such cues may be lost.
Grok	The word 'grok' was invented by Heinlein for his 1961 novel *Stranger in a Strange Land*, and roughly translated means 'understand'. It has a sense of deep comprehension and empathy as well as a cerebral understanding. The term has become part of the English language, included in dictionaries and used most by computer hackers.

Term/abbreviation	Meaning
ICT	ICT is used for 'Information and Communication Technology'. It is a term generally used in education circles to reflect the ever widening impact of Information Technology on knowledge, learning and skills.
IM&T	The term IM&T was coined for the 1992 NHS Information Strategy, and stands for 'Information Management and Technology'. Professor Dennis Protti of Victoria, British Colombia credits this as the first time a national health information strategy recognises the importance of information management alongside Information Technology.
IT	IT stands for 'Information Technology'. In this book, it is generally used to refer to the use of computer technology for presentation graphics in support (or not!) of public speaking.
Methodist	The Methodist movement is a Christian denomination with a tradition of placing preaching at the heart of its ministry. This includes preaching by lay people known as local preachers. The origin of the name is actually an insult applied to its founder and some of his friends in the 18th century.
Minimalism	Minimalism is used to describe movements in various forms of art and design, where the work is stripped down to its most fundamental features. As a historical movement in the arts it is identified with developments after World War II. It emerged as part of modernism, and is often associated with post-modernism. It is used in this book as a reaction against the over-elaborate use of presentation graphics, particularly animations.
Modernism	Modernism covers a variety of political, cultural and artistic movements which emerged rooted in the changes in Western society at the end of the 19th century and beginning of the 20th century. Historically, it can be interpreted as a trend of thought which affirms the ability of human beings to make, improve and reshape their environment, with the aid of scientific knowledge, technology and practical experimentation. In this book, it is used to represent the reshaping of public speaking by the use of computer (and other) technology.
NHS	The NHS is the UK's National Health Service.
NIMSAD	NIMSAD stands for 'Normative Information Model-based Systems Analysis and Design'. Glad that's clear. It is a framework developed by Professor Nimal Jayaratna to evaluate Information Systems Development methodologies. That's probably no better, so instead I'll refer you back to the picture in the text!
Oscar style	This term is used in the text to refer to the sort of speech given by Hollywood celebrities at the annual Awards ceremony of the American Film Academy known as the Oscars. They go on for ever, thank absolutely everybody, say very little and in some cases are accompanied by floods of tears!

Term/abbreviation	Meaning
PhD	A PhD is a Doctor of Philosophy postgraduate degree known commonly as a doctorate: it features on some of my slides.
Post-modernism	Post-modernism is a grossly over-used term used to describe a multitude of trends in the arts, philosophy, religion, technology, and many other fields that come after and deviate from modernism. It is used in the text precisely in this way, to describe what has, or should, come after the modernist style of public speaking. However, the text absolutely rejects the generally held view that the post-modernist approach means anything goes. On the contrary, it emphasises that spontaneity requires even more careful planning than ordered conformity.
PowerPoint	PowerPoint is the name of a proprietary product of the Microsoft Corporation. It has, however, followed Hoover into common parlance as a catch-all for presentation graphics software. For the record, it was not the first nor initially the most popular with Harvard Graphics, and then Freelance Graphics, being more popular in the early days, but PowerPoint rose to prominence through its inclusion in the Microsoft Office suite. These days, OpenOffice offers a perfectly good alternative, which is available for free. None of the techniques described in the text are specific to PowerPoint, but where detailed steps are described they are based on PowerPoint running on a PC platform.
Presentation graphics	In generic terms, presentation graphics refers to a type of software application that enables users to create stylised images for slide shows and reports. The software includes functions for creating various types of charts and graphs and for inserting text in a variety of fonts. The use of such software to replace photographic or overhead projection slides has led to individual pages being described as slides, and groups of pages as slideshows.
Readability	Readability is a rather ugly word used to describe the ease with which text or images can be read. There are measures of readability, but these should only be used as a guide as readability is a much more complex issue and is sensitive to audience and context.
Slide	The use of presentation graphics software to replace photographic or overhead projection slides has led to individual pages being described as slides, and this reflects the way the term is used in the text.
Slideshow	The use of presentation graphics software to replace photographic or overhead projection slides has led to groups of pages being described as slideshows, and this reflects the way the term is used in the text.

Term/abbreviation	Meaning
Texting	Another rather ugly term, used to describe the sending of text messages from mobile phones. Personally it reminds me of the Smash adverts for instant mashed potatoes in the early 1970s:
	First they design phones to talk to each other, Then they design phones that can be taken with them, Then they use tiny keypads to send text messages instead, And try to talk to desk-based computers with perfectly good keyboards!
	Paraphrase of the television advert voted UK public's all-time favourite
UCLAN	UCLAN is the University of Central Lancashire, based in Preston: it features on some of my slides.
URL	URL stands for Uniform Resource Locator, the global address of documents and other resources on the World Wide Web.
Venn Diagram	A Venn Diagram is made up of two or more overlapping circles. It is often used in mathematics to show relationships between sets. The overlapping area represents the intersection where both defining conditions are true.

Handout 4: Be inclusive: stay legal

Since the Disability Discrimination Act was introduced in 1999, all providers of goods and services have a legal obligation to avoid discrimination against disabled people in the way services or education are provided. Discrimination can take place in two ways – by treating a disabled person less favourably; and/or by failing to make 'reasonable adjustments' so that disabled people can participate in employment and education or make use of a service.

Besides, if you are in the business of communication, surely you want to be inclusive? Research tells us that just over 10% of the population of the United Kingdom have some form of disability (*source*: RNIB).

Much of the attention in the electronic arena has focused on websites, but the law applies to all activities. You can address the accessibility of your talk in a number of ways . . .

One very good reason for using a microphone when speaking is where a system is in place to help people with hearing aids. A loop system can make a talk accessible to many people with a hearing disability.

However, you can use other components of the talk to ensure that your messages are accessible, particularly presentation graphics and handouts. When considering such components of your talk, you should consider how they can be used to include people, and to ensure that you do not exclude anyone.

The main text highlighted the importance of simple slides and good contrast between text and the background.

For handouts, follow the RNIB clear print guidance. Clear print is a design approach which considers the needs of people with sight problems. Simply, a clear print document will find a wider audience. The solutions proposed are straightforward and inexpensive, focusing on some basic design elements, for example font, type size, contrast and page navigation.

1 The size of the type (known as point size) is a fundamental factor in legibility. We recommend a type size between 12 and 14 point (equivalent to a minimum x-height of 2mm or more ideally 2.3mm). The larger the minimum type size, the more people you will reach.
2 The better the contrast between the background and the text, the more legible the text will be. Note that the contrast will be affected by the size and weight of the type. Black text on a white background provides best contrast.
3 Avoid highly stylised typefaces, such as those with ornamental, decorative or handwriting styles.
4 Blocks of capital letters, underlined or italicised text are all harder to read. A word or two in capitals is fine but avoid the use of capitals for continuous text. Underlining text or setting it in italics should always be avoided and an alternative method of emphasis used.
5 The space between one line of type and the next (known as leading) is important. As a general rule, the space should be 1.5 to 2 times the space between words on a line.

6 People with sight problems often prefer bold or semi-bold weights to normal ones. Avoid light type weights.

7 If you print documents with numbers in them, choose a typeface in which the numbers are clear. Readers with sight problems can easily misread 3, 5, 8 and 0.

8 Keep to the same amount of space between each word. Do not condense or stretch lines of type. We recommend aligning text to the left margin as it is easy to find the start of the next line and keeps the spaces even between words. We advise that you avoid justified text as the uneven word spacing can make reading more difficult.

9 Make sure the margin between columns clearly separates them. If space is limited, use a vertical rule.

10 If using white type, make sure the background colour is dark enough to provide sufficient contrast.

11 Avoid fitting text around images if this means that lines of text start in a different place, and are therefore difficult to find. Set text horizontally as text set vertically is extremely difficult for a partially sighted reader to follow. Avoid setting text over images or textures as this will affect the contrast.

12 Partially sighted people tend to have handwriting that is larger than average, so allow extra space on forms. This will also benefit people with conditions that affect the use of their hands, such as arthritis.

13 It is helpful if recurring features, such as headings and page numbers, are always in the same place. A contents list and rules to separate different sections are also useful. Leave a space between paragraphs as dividing the text up gives the eye a break and makes reading easier.

14 Avoid glossy paper because glare makes it difficult to read. Choose uncoated paper that weighs over 90gsm. As a general rule, if the text is showing through from the reverse side, then the paper is too thin.

RNIB Clear Print Guidelines

There are many people who whilst not blind have visual impairments of various degrees. There is no point in going to the trouble of producing a handout if it doesn't enable you to communicate with your audience. In cases where you are dealing with people who are totally blind, a little planning could enable the handout to be translated into Braille.

For presentation slides, points 1 to 11 and 13 apply just as much as to printed handouts.

And if the use of a checklist seems very modernist, then simply go back and check the presentation graphics shown in the book. They are designed to be accessible and readable to a maximum number of people: accessible is not boring, and post-modern is not cluttered and chaotic.

Another relatively common problem is colour blindness. Estimates show that 8–12% of males have a significant degree of colour blindness:

• Deuteranomaly (5% of males): Deuteranomalous people are considered 'green weak'. Similar to the protanomalous person, they are poor at discriminating small differences in hues in the red, orange, yellow, green region of the spectrum. They make errors in the naming of hues in this region because they appear somewhat shifted towards red for them – difficulty in distinguishing violet from blue. From a practical standpoint though, many protanomalous and deuteranomalous people breeze through life with very little difficulty doing tasks that require normal colour vision. Some may not even be aware that their colour perception is in any way different from normal. The only problem they have is passing a colour vision test.

- Dicromasy can be divided into protanopia and deuteranopia (2% of males): These individuals normally know they have a colour vision problem and it can affect their lives on a daily basis. They see no perceptible difference between red, orange, yellow and green. All these colours that seem so different to the normal viewer appear to be the same colour for this 2% of the population.
- Protanopia (1% of males): For the protanope, the brightness of red, orange and yellow is much reduced compared to normal. This dimming can be so pronounced that reds may be confused with black or dark grey, and red traffic lights may appear to be extinguished. They may learn to distinguish reds from yellows and from greens primarily on the basis of their apparent brightness or lightness, not on any perceptible hue difference. Violet, lavender and purple are indistinguishable from various shades of blue because their reddish components are so dimmed as to be invisible, e.g. pink flowers, reflecting both red light and blue light, may appear just blue to the protanope.
- Deuteranopia (1% of males): The deuteranope suffers the same hue discrimination problems as the protanope, but without the abnormal dimming. The names red, orange, yellow and green really mean very little to him aside from being different names that everyone else around him seems to be able to agree on. Similarly, violet, lavender, purple and blue seem to be too many names to use logically for hues that all look alike to him.

Adapted from information supplied by Terrance L Waggoner, OD,
Staff Naval Hospital, Pensacola, FL.

So why all the space and big words devoted to this topic? Well, I should declare a personal interest. I am a green weak, deuteranomalous person. More importantly, I have personal experience of what happens if a speaker does not realise or take account of this apparently mild disability.

At school, when we covered the input/output characteristics of the humble transistor, my teacher put one on the board in yellow chalk and one in green. They looked exactly the same to me, so the lesson made little sense. It was half way through before I twigged they were meant to be different!

Handout 5: Further developments

By the time the book is published, the material should have been incorporated into an e-learning course, delivered through the Open Source virtual learning environment, Moodle. Intended to be a training resource for organisations, the e-learning course will add extra features making hopefully appropriate use of the technology.

For more information email me at <u>talking@alangillies.com</u>.

In the meantime here's a sneak preview:

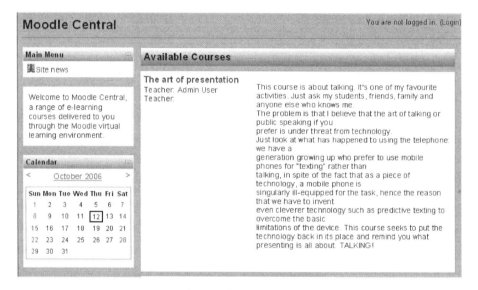

The introductory screen.

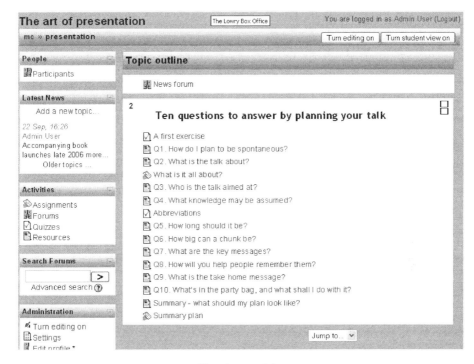

Planning module.

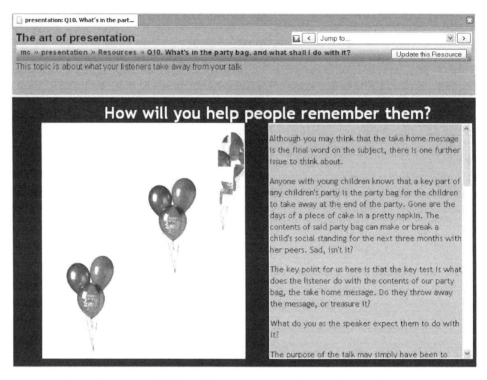

Sample teaching materials about what your listeners do with the take-home message.

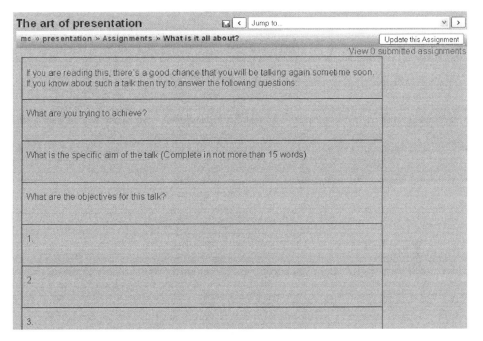

A sample exercise within the e-learning course.

Handout 6: Further reading and resources

Adams D. *The Hitchhiker's Guide to the Galaxy.* London: Pan Books; 1978.

Benner P. *From Novice to Expert: excellence and power in clinical nursing practice.* Menlo Park, CA: Addison Wesley; 1984.

Dreyfus SE, Dreyfus HL. *A five-stage model of the mental activities involved in skill acquisition.* Unpublished report supported by the Air Force Office of Scientific Research. Berkeley, CA: USAF, University of California; 1980.

Fraser J, Cave R. *Presenting in Biomedicine: 500 tips for success.* Oxford: Radcliffe Publishing; 2004.

Gillies AC. *Presenting Health with PowerPoint.* Oxford: Radcliffe Publishing; 2003.

Heinlein RA. *Stranger in a Strange Land.* London: Hodder & Stoughton; 1961, reprinted 2005.

Hart A. *Making Sense of Statistics in Healthcare.* Oxford: Radcliffe Publishing; 2001.

Storey L, Howard J, Gillies AC. *Competency in Healthcare.* Oxford: Radcliffe Publishing; 2002.

Index

abbreviations 16, 97–100
accessibility of presentations 101–3
acronyms 16, 97–100
Adams, Douglas 6
aims and objectives 11–12, 94
    see also key messages
anecdotes 40–1
animation use 21, 78, 83
appearance considerations 30–4
Arial font 21
arm waving 23–4, 35–6
audiences
    identification and targeting 12–15, 94
    participation exercises 24
    prior knowledge levels 15–17, 94
    question and answer sessions 48–50
    varying perspectives 45–7

background graphics 21, 78, 83
bar charts 66–8
Benner, P 4–5
body language 7, 35–6
Braille 102
breathing exercises 42
'building-up' concepts 60–2
bullet points 3, 57–60

checklists 31
'chunks' of information 20–2
colour blindness 102–3
colour use 21, 77, 82
computers see information technology (IT)
controversial statements 6
cultural considerations
    facial expressions and gaze 37
    use of humour 39

data presentations 64–8
deception 37
demonstrations 23–4
detail of presentations 50–1
    tiered approaches 68–70
deuteranomaly 102–3
deuteranopia 103
diagrams 21, 77, 82
dicromasy 103
disability considerations 101–3
dress styles 31–4
Dreyfus, SE and Dreyfus, HL 4–5
'drying up' 36

expertise development, processes involved 4–5
eye gaze 37
eye sight problems 101–3

facial expressions 37, 38
Flesch Reading Ease formula 13
Flesch-Kincaid Grade Level scores 13
'fluffy cloud' graphics 57–9
follow-up information sources 26–7, 96
fonts 21, 76, 81
    and vision problems 101–2

graphics see presentation graphics
graphs and charts 64–8
'Grok' 39, 97

hand gestures 35–8
handouts 96
Hart, Anna 65
Heinlein, RA 39, 97
humour use 37–40
    and visual images 63–4

identifying target audiences 12–15, 94
information technology (IT), drawbacks 2–3,
    10–11

jargon use 16–17
jokes 37–40

key messages 22–3, 95
    reinforcement strategies 23–4, 45–7, 73–83
    and 'take-home' points 25–7, 89–90
    use of images 62–4
    see also message delivery
King, Martin Luther 1

language and terminology
    addressing audience needs 15–17
    avoiding misunderstandings 15–17
    non-native speakers 87–8
learning styles 23, 45
legibility issues
    font types 21, 76, 81
    graphs and data presentations 67, 82
    and vision problems 101–2
length of presentations 17–19, 95
list styles 57–60
listeners see audiences
loop systems 101

message delivery
  detail and content considerations 50–1,
    68–70
  identifying audience needs 12–17, 94
  key points 22–3, 95
  length issues 17–20, 95
  level of detail 50–1
  pace considerations 17–19, 41–3
  packaging in 'chunks' 20–2
  reinforcement strategies 23–4, 45–7, 73–83
  take-home and follow-up issues 25–7, 89–90
microphone use 101
'milestone' images 70–3
monotone deliveries 44

nervousness
  mannerisms 35–6
  and speaking pace 18, 41–3
non-native speakers 87–8
non-verbal communication 7
  facial expressions 37, 38
  hand gestures 35–8
  and physical actions 23–4

Open Source learning 104–7
Oscar style 98

pace of presentations 17–19, 41–3
partially sighted people 101–2
pauses 43
physical actions 23–4
pie charts 65, 67
pitch and tone of speech 43–4
planning approaches 9–11
poor presentation skills 1–2
  and IT 3–4
'post-modernism' 7, 99
PowerPoint 99
pre-reading 96
presentation graphics 99
  drawbacks 10–11
  minimalist approaches 53–5
  rationing use 7–8
  as 'signposts' 70–3
  staging explanations 60–2
  timing of use 56–7
  using bullets and clouds 57–60
  using packages 3
  using visual images 23, 62–8
presentation skills
  pre-modern era 1–2
  modern era 2–6
  post-modernism 6–8
  see also skills acquisition
presentations
  basic rules 20–1
  detail and content balances 50–1, 68–70
  key components 50–2, 96

making accessible 101–3
  style considerations 29–52, 74–83
  time and length issues 17–20, 95
  see also message delivery
Presenting Health with PowerPoint (Gillies)
    20–1
process building 60–2
protanopia 103

question and answer sessions 48–50

'readability' 99
readability scores 13
relaxation techniques 41–2
repeat phrases 36
repetitions, message reinforcement aids
    73–83
Reynolds, Malvina 3
'rules' of communication 4–6
  when to break 7–8

signposting graphics
  'milestone' images 70–3
  'warning' sign images 73–83
skills acquisition, processes involved 4–5
slide presentations
  basic rules 20–1
  content of slides 79–83
  minimalist approaches 53–5
  style considerations 21, 57–68, 74–83
  timing issues 18–19, 56–7
  usefulness 22
  as 'warm-up' acts 84–7
  see also presentation graphics
'sound-bites' 20
speaking pace 18, 41–3
speaking volume 43–4
spontaneity 9–11
Storey, L et al. 4–5
story-telling 40–1
Stranger in a Strange Land (Heinlein) 39
stress reactions 35–6
  and relaxation techniques 41–2
subject matter, planning approaches 11–12

take-home messages 25–7, 89–90
technology and presentations, impact on quality
    1, 3–4
'texting' 100
think bubbles 57–60
timekeeping 17–19
Times New Roman font 21
tone of delivery 44
topics, planning issues 11–12

upper case 21, 76, 81
USA audiences 16

verbal messages 23
video recordings 24
vision problems, presentation considerations
    101–3
visual images 23, 62–8
  as 'warm-up' act 84–7
voice
  tone and pitch 44

volume of delivery 43–4

'warm-up' acts 84–7
Wesley, John 1
Wilde, Oscar 6

Yes Prime Minister (BBC) 30